GOD'S
YARDSTICK

Library of Congress Catalog Card No. 80-70235
ISBN 0-934874-02-6
Printed in the U.S.A.

GOD'S YARDSTICK

By
Gerard Berghoef
Lester De Koster

Christian's Library Press
Grand Rapids, Michigan

This volume is adapted from the
authors' *Deacons Handbook.*

THE AUTHORS

Mr. Gerard Berghoef is a native of the Netherlands, who emigrated to the United States early in the 1950s. He is presently a furniture manufacturing executive, and has served the Christian Reformed Church as an elder for twelve years.

Dr. Lester DeKoster is a native of Michigan, and has been professor of speech and director of the library for Calvin College and Seminary, Grand Rapids, Michigan. He retired in 1980 as Editor of *The Banner*, official weekly publication of the Christian Reformed Church.

The authors have previously published *The Elders Handbook*, A Practical Guide for Church Leaders, and *The Deacons Handbook*, a Manual of Stewardship.

The authors are grateful to our wives,
Audrey Berghoef and Ruth DeKoster
for wise counsel and persistent support.

TO THE READER...

What should we do with what we are given? It's a question Christians ask.

Given, that is, by God who is the author of life, and time, and talent, and all creation.

Life is God's gift. So is time, the form in which life passes from cradle to grave, from birth to judgment.

How shall we use life and time through the fleeting hours that we have them?

What will we do with the talents implanted in each of us by God? Why has He given each of us just that unique combination of skills and potential which makes every human being different from every other (there are no second editions in the human race, none at all!)?

How should we use the goods our efforts acquire? Is all that we earn ours to use as we please? If not, how much may we keep for ourselves? What do we owe the Lord, and our neighbor?

These and similar questions come to focus in the term "stewardship".

We invite you to explore with us the meaning of stewardship as taught by the Scriptures. We urge you to react to what is said, and to search the Bible for yourself to see if what we urge upon you is true. And we suggest that you discuss stewardship with friends, in Bible study groups, and Church societies.

All because we believe that stewardship is what the Christian life is all about.

"Let your loins be girded and your lamps
burning, and be like men who are waiting
for their master to come home from the
marriage feast, so that they may open to
him at once when he comes and knocks.
Blessed are those servants whom the
master finds awake when he comes; truly,
I say to you, he will gird himself and have
them sit at table, and he will come and
serve them. If he comes in the second
watch, or in the third, and finds them so,
blessed are those servants!"
"Peter said, 'Lord, are you telling this parable for us or for all?' And the Lord said,
'Who then is the faithful and wise steward, whom his master will set over his
household, to give them their portion of
food at the proper time? Blessed is that
servant whom his master when he comes
will find so doing.'" (Luke 12:35-38; 41-43)

TABLE OF CONTENTS

To The Reader

Table of Contents

Introduction

Chapter:

1. The Forms Of Stewardship 15

2. The Fundamentals Of Stewardship . . . 22

3. What May I Keep For Myself? 39

4. Why Give At All? 49

5. Why Give Money And Goods? 54

6. Stewardship Through The Church's
   Deacons 57

7. How Much?
   (From Mites To Millions) 68

8. Sacrifice And Stewardship 75

9. Levels Of Awareness:
   Faith And Works 85

10. God And Conscience 94

11. The Mystery Of Poverty 102

12. The Mystery Of Wealth 112

13. Parables For Stewards 149

14. Stewardship In The Welfare State . . . 164

15. Social Structures And Human Need:
    Marxism, Liberation Theology 173

16. The Church And The International
    Community 179

In A Nutshell 182

Epilog 183

Introduction

A yardstick measures the unknown by a fixed standard.

Yardsticks may be applied under various circumstances and in varied ways—but always for the same purpose, namely to see how the unknown measures up.

God has His yardstick, to measure our behavior.

We do not have to show God how much we love Him. He knows.

His yardstick is for testing ourselves so that we may know whether our love for Him, as expressed in our love for our neighbors, is genuine and growing.

God's yardstick is what the Scriptures teach concerning Christian use of the life, time, talents and goods which God entrusts to us.

Our limited lease upon God's gifts runs for a time He has fixed. Then comes the judgment foretold in the Lord's parable: "Now after a long time the master of those servants came and settled accounts with them..." (Matt. 25:18).

God's yardstick is a preview of the standards used in that final settlement of accounts with each of us.

This book is an effort to discern the divine measuring rod in God's Word—and to assist us all in applying it to our use of His gifts.

Nothing could be more important, for the right use of the talents and the pounds God gives us is what life is finally all about.

Chapter 1.
THE FORMS OF STEWARDSHIP

Stewardship is far more than the handling of our money. Stewardship is the handling of life, and time, and destiny.

Money does indeed do many things. Using our money as good stewards is certainly one of the severest tests of our citizenship in His Kingdom.

But stewardship extends beyond giving money.

A. *THE COMMON FORMS*

The forms which stewardship assumes are defined, first of all, by the human needs we encounter. And the needs we meet are the needs which we in fact become aware of. Be assured that God provides a need, within reach, for every talent, every skill, every gift of any kind which He gives us. It is simply hardness of heart which blinds the eye, closes the ear, and lames the limbs when opportunities for good stewardship are unobserved.

Like the pussy cat who went to London, in the fable, for to see the Queen, but who saw only a mouse beneath her throne, so we perceive in the world about us—beginning at home—only what we have the heart bent on encountering. A heart softened by grace and beating, now, in tune with divine love finds opportunities for stewardship in direct proportion to the gifts which God has given for that purpose. Gift and need are divinely matched. The need may, in fact, alert us to gifts we did not know we had.

The basic forms of stewardship are twice defined: 1) by the opportunities for doing good that we learn to become aware of, and 2) by the gifts God has on deposit with us designed to meet such opportunities.

The Bible puts the basic forms of stewardship within everyone's reach by speaking in terms of cups of cold water, going an extra mile, crusts of bread, a helping hand, the exercise of patience, and the like. Make a list sometime of the very ordinary forms of stewardship the Bible asks of us. It will become clear that basic stewardship is concerned with sweetening human relationships in our everyday world. Nothing momentous. Something like a genuine smile, nod, wave, kindly word, the steadying hand; and the sensitive heart, compassionate spirit, flowing out into acts of kindness, generosity, trust, grace. Time invested in these virtues is time invested in heaven. None is beyond our reach—if the heart be aware, and the will bent to do God's service wherever and whenever...!

B. *SPECIAL FORMS*

Some aspects of stewardship are defined by the extent of the gifts God entrusts to us.

Has He given you wealth? Steward it in service of the needy, both in kind and by way of the influence which wealth gives.

Has He given you position? Fill it gracefully and for the good of all those whose lives you affect.

Has He given you talents of various kinds? Use yours for the benefit of the community.

Whatever the uncommon gift, it is given to serve. So steward it!

C. *WORK*

The basic form of stewardship is daily work. No matter what that work may be. No matter if you have never before looked upon your job as other than a drudge, a bore, a fearful trial. Know that the harder it is for you to face each working day, the more your will to persevere schools the soul.

Work is the fundamental form of stewardship because:

1. *God Himself works:* "My Father worketh and I work" (John 5:17), the Lord says. It is not recounted that God plays, but He works.

That is to say, God is ever busy making provision for our existence. Work is that which
serves another. Play is that which serves ourselves.

2. *Work knits the fabric of civilization.* We
take for granted all the possibilities which
work alone provides. And we become aware of
how work sustains the order which makes life
possible when that order is rent by lightning
flashes of riot or war, and the necessities which
work normally provides become difficult to
come by.

3. *Man's history begins in a garden and
mounts to a city.* A garden is what God the
Holy Spirit does, without man, with a wilderness. A city is what God the Holy Spirit does
through man's work.

4. *It is of the nature of work to serve the
community.* Whether work be done in the
home, on the land, or in the countless forms of
enterprise developed across the centuries,
work is doubly blessed: a) it provides for the
family of man, and b) it matures the worker.

5. *Work matures the worker because it requires ethical decision.* Merely to rise to one's
daily tasks requires an act of will, a decision to
serve the community, however reluctantly,
however unaware the worker may be that such
is the case. Such willed acts of service not only
make and sustain the fabric of civilization and
culture, but also develop the soul. And, while
the object of work is destined to perish, the

soul formed by daily decision to do work carries over into eternity.

6. *This perspective on work,* as a maturing of the soul, *liberates the believer* from undue concern over the monotony of the assembly line, the threat of technology, or the reduction of the worker to but an easily replaceable cog in the industrial machine. One's job may be done by another. But each doer is himself unique, and what carries over beyond life and time is not the work but the worker. What doing the job does for each of us is not repeated in anyone else. What the exercise of will, of tenacity, of courage, of foresight, of triumph over temptations to get by, does for you is uniquely your own. One worker may replace another on the assembly line, but what each worker carries away from meeting the challenge of doing the day's shift will ever be his own. The lasting and creative consequence of daily work happens to the worker. God so arranges that civilization grows out of the same effort that develops the soul.

7. *The forms of work are countless,* but the typical one is *work with the hands.* The Bible has reference to the sower, to the making of tents and of things out of clay, to tilling the fields and tending the vine. Hand work makes visible the plan in the mind, just as the deed makes visible the love in the heart. While the classic Greek mind tended to scorn work with the hands, the Bible suggests that something about it structures the soul.

8. *The results of one's work can never be fully known.* What will become of the produce raised, of the machine built, of the person fed? No one can foretell what will be the final consequence of today's effort. Nor does the pay check really measure the value, nor the effort, of the work for which it is given. Wages are set by the market, and the results of work are hidden in the mists of tomorrow. What endures is what happens to the worker who bravely makes it through the day.

9. *Seen in this light,* which is the light shed by the Bible upon work, *it is easy to understand why work is the primary form of stewardship.* To work most of us give the largest unit of our lives. By work we together raise the level of our culture, keep its order, supply its needs, and point to its promise of better living for more of the world's peoples.

10. *For the believer, then, stewardship begins with the day's work.* Done well, as unto God, in the full knowledge that by work the world lives, work serves God and man and the self.

D. *PLAY*

We have spoken of play as that which is done to please or serve the self. Play may absorb much effort, long planning, and lots of time. But so long as the end in view is the satisfaction of the self, such effort cannot be called work. This is true whatever the form of play, whatever its esteem in the community as compared with work. What the self heaps up in time for its own use does not carry over into eternity, and burdens the soul which is thus occupied.

Play may be indulged as recreation, that is as preparation for doing work better when the worker has been so refreshed.

You will know whether it is work, or play, which is occupying your time, your effort, and...your life. And knowing, you can yourself judge whether the time and effort you give to any activity is work, an investment in eternity, or play, an investment in temporality.

Chapter 2.
THE FUNDAMENTALS OF STEWARDSHIP

The practice of stewardship is the supreme challenge of the Christian life. The Bible makes stewardship the key to Christian behavior.

A. *THE STEWARD*

Who is a steward?
What is a steward?
Eliezer was steward over the vast household of Abraham. That is to say, Eliezer was in charge of all that Abraham had (Gen. 24:1).

Joseph was steward of the household of Potiphar, officer of Pharoah, who "put him in charge of all that he had" (Gen. 39:4).

The steward owns nothing and governs everything. To him the master commits control of all that he possesses. Of all, that is, of the master's material goods. This high and responsible office, mentioned in the first book of the Bible, appears still in the parables of Jesus: "There was a rich man who had a steward..." (Luke 16:1); "And when evening came, the owner of the vineyard said to his steward..." (Matt. 20:8).

"It is required of stewards," St. Paul writes of his own calling, "that they be found trustworthy" (I Cor. 4:2).

And St. Peter applies the concept of stewardship to the Christian life, saying: "As each has received a gift, employ it for one another, as good stewards of God's varied grace: whoever speaks, as one who utters oracles of God; whoever renders service, as one who renders it by the strength which God supplies; in order that in everything God may be glorified through Jesus Christ" (I Pet. 4:10-11).

The parables of the talents (Matt. 25:14-30) and of the pounds (Luke 19:11-27) show that the steward will be required to render account of all that has been placed under his stewardship.

God makes man steward of His world. Who is man, asks the Psalmist? And answers: "Thou hast made him little less than God, and dost crown him with glory and honor. Thou hast given him dominion over the works of thy hands; thou hast put all things under his feet..." (Ps. 8:5-6).

God makes man the master of His temporal household. Like all stewards, man is not the owner. He is the overseer. For three score years and ten, more or less as the case may be, each of us is steward over those talents and those pounds alloted us by divine Providence.

And at the end comes the accounting: "Now after a long time the master of those servants came and settled accounts with them..." (Matt. 25:19); "When he returned, having received the kingly power, he commanded those servants to whom he had given the money, to be called to him, that he might know what they had gained by trading..." (Luke 19:15).

As each has managed his stewardship, so will he be judged: "Well done, good servant," or, "But as for these enemies of mine, who did not want me to reign over them, bring them here and slay them before me" (Luke 19:17, 27).

The quality of stewardship depends upon obedience to the master's will. The steward who does not obey the master's law rejects the master's authority and serves another.

Our stewardship is the test: do we mean to serve God or Mammon, the Lord or the Devil?

Stewardship is, we repeat, key to the Christian life—and death, and judgment.

B. *BASIC PRINCIPLES OF STEWARDSHIP*

The fundamentals of stewardship as revealed in the Scriptures are briefly stated:

1. All things are made and sustained by God: "In the beginning God created the heavens and the earth" (Gen. 1:1). "The earth is the Lord's and the fulness thereof, the world and those who dwell therein..." (Ps. 24:1). "Behold," says Moses, "to the Lord your God

belong heaven and the heaven of heavens, the earth with all that is in it..." (Deut. 10:14). All is God's, including man himself. This is the first and most basic fundamental of stewardship. It is a truth of revelation that we must never forget!

2. God also gives and sustains human life, as He sets man within His world: "Then the Lord God formed man of dust from the ground, and breathed into his nostrils the breath of life; and man became a living soul" (Gen. 2:7). "In his hand is the life of every living thing and the breath of all mankind" (Job 12:10). God gives us life, and time, and a world in which to live it! Still all is from Him. Christian, remember!

3. God decides when to terminate the life He gives: "Thou turnest man back to the dust, and sayest, 'Turn back, O children of men!'" (Ps. 90:3). And God sustains all the moments between birth and death: "My times are in thy hand" (Ps. 31:15).

4. God determines upon the distribution of goods received by each during his lifetime: "The Lord makes poor and makes rich; he brings low, he also exalts" (I Sam. 2:7). What each of us has to steward, what each receives as talent or pound, is wholly from God! Everyone believes that whatever he has was acquired by the sweat of his own brow or the shrewdness of his own wit. But this is not what the Scripture teaches: "Beware lest you say in your heart, 'My power and the might of my

hand have gotten me this wealth.' You shall remember the Lord your God, for it is he who gives you power to get wealth" (Deut. 8:17). There are no self-made men; there are only God-made men! All that we have is His gift! "The blessing of Jehovah, it maketh rich..." (Prov. 10:22). The steward must first of all know whose goods they are which he administers, and recognize that whatever he has in his hands comes to him from the Master. Not to know this is to risk idolatry, as the Prophet says to Israel: "And she did not know that it was I who gave her the grain, the wine, and the oil, and who lavished upon her silver and gold which they used for Baal" (Hos. 2:8). It is pagan to think that things come by chance. It is self-idolatry to think that possessions come by our own earning. It is Christian to know that all we have comes as a gift of God. This knowledge, too, is basic to right understanding of stewardship. Indeed, if we owned that which we are called to steward, we would no longer be stewards but masters!

5. Because He is creator, owner, and master of all, God alone sets the requirements for stewardship of His goods and world. Between Himself and those who would be His faithful stewards, God makes covenant: "Listen to my voice, and do all that I command you. So shall you be my people, and I will be your God" (Jer. 11:4).

6. The revealed law governing stewardship

comes to expression in the Ten Commandments. The meaning of the Commandments is expounded by the Prophets. It is repeated by Jesus Christ, and applied by the Apostles. The whole Bible is the book of this covenant: "...do all that I command you. So shall you be my people, and I will be your God." Our Lord sums up the law and the prophets in a sentence: "So whatever you wish that men would do to you, do so to them; for this is the law and the prophets" (Matt. 7:12).

7. To every steward there open two ways: "Enter by the narrow gate; for the gate is wide and the way is easy, that leads to destruction, and those who enter by it are many. For the gate is narrow and the way is hard, that leads to life, and those who find it are few" (Matt. 7:13-14).

8. And finally, both ways come to judgment: "And I saw the dead, great and small, standing before the throne, and books were opened. Also another book was opened, which is the book of life. And the dead were judged by what was written in the books, by what they had done" (Rev. 20:12). The Bible opens with the days of creation and ends with the day of judgment. And between them lies, for every one, the period of stewardship, when God makes each of us responsible for the use of His gifts according to His directions.

These are the fundamentals of the doctrine of stewardship. They explain why stewardship is key to the Christian life.

C. *SUMMARY*

Let us summarize briefly, now, the basics of stewardship:

1. God creates, sustains, and thus owns all things, man included. Not only in the beginning, but always. Every child born into the world receives life from God.

2. God brings us to life within His vast and beautiful and challenging world, and permits us to use and enjoy all that He sustains.

3. He intends, however, that His will shall govern our wills and His desires control our desires. He reveals His will in the inspired Scriptures. As we walk in His world, His law shall be lamp to our feet and light upon our path (Ps. 119:105).

4. Our use of God's property, whether as faithful or rebellious stewards, is, therefore, what life is all about.

5. Our obedience, or disobedience, to God's will revealed in His Word becomes the basis for the Last Judgment, prelude to heaven or hell.

D. *DIFFICULTIES: CREATION*

The basic tenets of stewardship can give rise to problems and objections which believers may meet. We discuss some of them here:

1. The doctrine of creation is, of course, confronted by the theory of evolution. This theory

is now advocated with far less assurance than once it was, but it still sets the secular trend. Christians cannot hope to demonstrate the truth of creationism before they act upon the truth of stewardship. Without engaging in endless dispute, the believer wisely proceeds upon faith in the Scriptures. God is creator. Man, too, is His creation, not only the first man, but each and every person born into the world. Whether or not the Biblical account permits an interpretation which allows for long periods of time in the process of creation, the crux of the issue is that *God made all that is,* that He made man in His own Image, and that man, made perfect, chose to disobey and fall into sin. All this is revelation. All else is speculation. Far better to take the Word at what it says than lose the truth and clarity of Genesis in a haze of shifting "science".

2. Do not be misled, either, by secular depreciations of the earth as but a tiny speck of dust lost in an immense universe. Remember that Genesis teaches that God spoke the universe into being. When the infinite and majestic God speaks, He says *something!* Small wonder that the glories of the starry skies stretch far beyond our comprehension. Are you surprised that galaxies and universes and mysteries happen when God speaks! Leave it to those of no faith to belittle man in comparison with the stars made expressly for man's delight. Recall that of all created things, only man is made in

God's Image: "...for God made man in His own image" (Gen. 9:6). And about the stars God says: "Lift up your eyes on high and see: who created these? He who brings out their host by number, calling them all by name; by the greatness of his might, and because he is strong in power not one is missing" (Is. 40:26). And, the Prophet goes on to say, far from demeaning us, let the wonder of the heavens excite our confidence in their Creator, for He is "the everlasting God, the creator of the ends of the earth. He does not faint or grow weary...He gives power to the faint, and to him who has no might he increases strength..." (Is. 40:28-29). The unending extent of space, the throbbing energy, the sparkling fire, the utter mystery— all these are not to demean us, but to awaken us to whose Image we bear and upon whose strength we can depend.

3. In making His universe, God lays down patterns of behavior to it. We call these patterns "natural law". Do not let natural law intrude between you and the active presence of God all about us. "My Father is working," our Lord says, "and I am working" (John 5:17). We call this working "natural law". God, not meteorology, sends the weather. God gives the leaves, awakens the sun, rides on the storm: "...to the snow he says, 'Fall on the earth'; and to the shower and the rain, 'Be strong'...By the breath of God ice is given, and the broad waters are frozen fast. He loads the thick cloud with moisture; the clouds scatter his lightning. They turn round and round by his guidance, to accomplish all that he commands them on the face of the habitable world" (Job 37:6, 10-12).

The doctrine of stewardship is impressed upon us by a vivid sense of God's immanent activity in all that we often take for granted or account as natural behavior.

E. *DIFFICULTIES: LIFE*

1. None chooses to be born. That is a decision made before birth. We did not ask for life. God gives it to us. Medicine employs all that is now known of "natural law" to prolong life against disease, but God numbers our days: "the number of his months is with thee, and thou hast appointed his bounds that he cannot pass" (Job 14:5). The time for the tests of stewardship is not ours to measure, nor enlarge: "And which of you by being anxious can add one cubit to his span of life?" (Matt. 6:27). The hoarding of goods which competes with stewardship roots in anxiety about the morrow, an anxiety our Lord rejects because our tomorrows are in God's hand.

2. The time and place of our birth, our family, race, talents, looks—all these are by God's design. Some are born to wealth; others see the light of day in the clutch of destitution. Where and how life is given is God's choice, our lot. Neither envy of the rich nor scorn for the poor befits our heritage, for where we were born was not of our choosing—and envy or scorn falls upon Him who made us.

F. *DIFFICULTIES: FREEDOM*

1. God holds us responsible for our stewardship because He has made us free. But freedom cannot be harmonized with "natural law". We are not patterned, as are the stars and the atoms, by a divine activity so consistent that we speak of it as "law". God respects the liberty of His Image-bearer. God does not invade the human spirit. Demons take possession if they can; God stands "at the door and knocks" (Rev. 3:20). With infinite delicacy, the Creator respects the integrity of the man He has made. But this cannot be explained. A freedom explained is not freedom, for explanation involves cause and effect. Freedom has no cause; it is a divine gift.

2. But the atoms of our bodies obey natural law. This is the foundation of medicine. Yet the self inter-twined with the flesh of the body is free. And because free, therefore responsible for the stewardship it exercises. This we do not explain; this we affirm: every command in the Scriptures assumes freedom.

3. The mystery of freedom is further complicated by the "mystery of iniquity" (II Thess. 2:7). How sin entered God's good creation is told us in Genesis (chapter 3). But explanation for sin there is none: "the mystery of iniquity." But as sinner, man lost an aspect of his freedom. No longer, after the defection of Adam, could man obey the law of stewardship simply through his own choice: "As it is written, 'None is righteous, no, not one; no one understands, no one seeks for God. All have turned aside, together they have gone wrong; no one does good, not even one'" (Rom. 3:10-12).

4. What fallen man, then, could not do for himself—properly use God's goods—Jesus Christ makes possible for us, dying for our sins that in Him we might have newness of life (Rom. 6:4), a newness manifest in stewardship —that is, in what the Bible calls good works: "For we are his workmanship, created in Christ Jesus for good works, which God prepared beforehand, that we should walk in them" (Eph. 2:10). Stewardship, freely chosen in accord with God's law, is possible in Christ Jesus. Not that our works save us (Rom. 3:28), but rather that we are saved for good works— that is, for stewardship.

G. *DIFFICULTIES: GETTING THE WORD*

1. How shall the law go forth? How shall mankind hear the demand for stewardship?

Through the Church. As explained in our *Elders Handbook,* God lays upon the Church the responsibility for educating in stewardship: "Go therefore and make disciples of all nations, baptizing them in the name of the Father and of the Son and of the Holy Spirit, teaching them to observe all that I have commanded you..." (Matt. 28:19-20). Observe from this passage, commonly called The Great Commission:

a. The mandate is given to the Apostles, founders of the New Testament Church.

b. Through them the Church is required to disciple all nations; a disciple being one who follows the teaching of a master. Believers are to be Christ's disciples, taken into the Church by baptism.

c. The Church is commanded to teach disciples to do all that the Lord has commanded; that is, teach all believers His application and interpretation of the law and the prophets —in other words, the governing principles of stewardship.

d. The primary task of the Church, then, is to proclaim the Word which generates new birth, and to teach the Word which governs the life of stewardship.

Obviously, Christian stewardship will be most successfully practiced whenever and wherever the Church most obediently is...the Church!

H. *DIFFICULTIES:*
WHAT LIFE IS ALL ABOUT

The meaning of life is the subject of endless speculation and confusion among those who fail to seek life's purpose from the Giver of life. Those looking for light on life from words other than the Word of God can find countless books, articles, lectures, study groups, exotic religions, gurus and "masters" crying out to confuse them. But only God knows why He gives us life, and time to use life, and all His gifts, along with the talents to employ them aright. And God tells....

In the Scriptures, and,

Through the Church, which He sustains for the purpose of teaching mankind from the Bible what life is, indeed, all about.

Life and time are God's primary gifts. To live is to have time. To have time is to live. Time enshrines what we do with life. There is no doing over. Past is past!

What our doing pours into the mold of time: this is what life is all about.

Whom our doing serves, God or mammon, the Lord's Word or the devil's lie: this is the crucial choice for which time gives life opportunity: "...choose this day whom you will serve..." (Josh. 24:15). Time always registers today. Today is always opportunity, and obligation, for choice: "But exhort one another every day, as long as it is called 'today,' that none of you may be hardened by the deceitfulness of sin" (Heb. 3:13). Jesus said, "We must work the works of him who sent me, while it is day; night comes, when no one can work" (John 9:4).

To live is to be confronted by choice. Choice emerges in doing. Time crystallizes deed, in testimony to the presence or absence of saving faith, in anticipation of the judgment.

Life is the God-given power to use the God-given gift of time in obedience to the Giver. Faith is the God-given power to obey the Word of the Lord instead of the interests of self or the words of unbelief: "choose this day..," for it is always "today" until the night comes!

I. *DIFFICULTIES: JUDGMENT*

If salvation is by faith, the free gift of God, why then the final judgment? "For God will bring every deed into judgment, with every secret thing, whether good or evil" (Eccles. 12:14). "And the dead were judged by what was written in the books, by what they had done" (Rev. 20:12). "For he will render to every man according to his works..." (Rom. 2:6).

How can this be if salvation is not by works but by faith: "For by grace you have been saved through faith; and this is not your own doing, it is the gift of God—not because of works, lest any man should boast" (Eph. 2:8-9)?

Every believer knows, in the depths of his heart, that he can no more earn heaven than climb the sky to reach it. We are not really surprised that the Bible rejects the notion that salvation is the reward of good works.

For what, then, are believers to be judged? It is undeniable that judgment upon our works does await us. Texts affirming that, like those already quoted, could be multiplied.

An answer to this difficulty is suggested by the miracles of Jesus. He made the blind to see, the deaf to hear, the lame to walk. He even made the dead alive again.

Why all this? Sometimes to validate the Lord's call for belief in Him (John 20:30-31), but also for another reason: to restore these crippled organs to use! That even the dead-made-alive could put the gift of life to use once more.

What once stood in the way of normal life was removed. The sick, and the deformed, and the demon-possessed were liberated by a Word from the Lord.

So the believer is today liberated by the same Word, through faith, from what stands in the way of a new life of obedience.

Take note of these things about the Lord's miracles:

1. The miracle is not an end in itself. Often it is followed by the Lord's own parting admonition: go, do! A handicap is gone. A life is restored. What then? How will the new freedom be used? The question then—the question now!

2. The Lord's healing usually came in response to faith: "Thy faith hath made thee whole" (Matt. 9:22). "And Jesus said to him. 'If you can! All things are possible to him who believes'" (Mark 9:23). Faith is commonly the road that miracles walk. Faith is the vehicle on which miracles ride. No less today then when

Jesus walked the earth.

3. Faith is the means to wholeness. Faith accepts newness of life. Faith enters upon liberation in Christ Jesus. And the new life, given through faith, reveals its presence in good works: "...by works was faith made perfect" (Jas. 2:22). The purpose of healing finds its goal in the obedient use of the body made new.

The miraculous restoration of life through faith, of liberation by faith, goes on now in every believer. Life dead in sin is raised by the Word to newness in obedience. Eyes blind to the presence of God in creation (Ps. 19:1), and to the presence of Christ in the needy, see once again. Ears deaf to the Word and to the cries of the oppressed now hear and inspire response. Limbs lamed by self-indulgence now are extended to serve the neighbor. All this as evidence that faith, true and saving faith, is indeed present; none of these if faith be dead: "So faith by itself, if it has no works, is dead" (Jas. 2:17).

The final judgment, being focused upon works, is passed upon the presence or absence of faith. By faith are we saved, as revealed by our works. By unfaith are we lost, as revealed by our works: "And the dead were judged...by what they had done," just because "by grace you have been saved through faith...."

Chapter 3.

WHAT MAY I KEEP FOR MYSELF?

How much of my goods, time, interests, talents do I owe the needy?

Or, how much of all that God gives me may I keep for, and use on, myself?

How does anyone answer such questions?

First, by putting them to the Scriptures. Second, by setting the Scriptural answers into his own time and place.

A. *THE SCRIPTURES*

The Bible never gives a dollar and cents answer to questions like these. The Bible functions through conscience (see Chapter 9, B). And to sensitize conscience, the Bible does suggest an investor's guide which the pulpit should be urged to apply frequently to the congregation, and which the prudent believer will apply to himself and assist others in applying to themselves.

Yes, an investor's guide!

It is simply this: give away to the needy all

the goods, time, talent, effort which you want to invest in heaven. Give to the needy whatever you want to reap beyond the grave. Keep for yourself whatever you don't want to see again in any form after your eyelids close for the last time.

The Bible serves conscience as an investor's manual. The prudent investor takes heed.

This is what the Lord teaches through His remarks to what is commonly called the rich young ruler: "Go, sell what you have, and give to the poor, and you will have treasure in heaven..." (Mark 10:21). The Lord thus confirms the inspired teaching of Proverbs: "He who is kind to the poor lends to the Lord, and he will repay him for his deed" (Prov. 19:17).

St. Paul compares heavenly investment with sowing seed which comes to fruition in eternity: "He who sows sparingly will also reap sparingly, and he who sows bountifully will also reap bountifully" (II Cor. 9:6). A stingy planting guarantees a poor harvest.

Believers must take the significance of this language of sowing and reaping very seriously. God does. The Spirit inspires the Apostle to say very plainly: "Do not be deceived; God is not mocked, for whatever a man sows, that he will also reap" (Gal. 6:7).

Lending to the Lord via giving to the poor is secure investment. It survives even death itself. It is, moreover, gilt-edged and blue-chip: "Give and it will be given to you; good measure, pressed down, shaken together, running over, will be put in your lap. For the measure you give will be the measure you get back," says the Lord Jesus (Luke 6:38). Again: "And he said to them, 'Take heed what you hear; the measure you give will be the measure you get, and still more will be given you'" (Mark 4:24).

This is why St. Paul molds the conscience in these words: "It is more blessed to give than to receive" (Acts 20:35), a saying he attributes to Jesus.

It is in this light that we all must understand the warnings in the Bible against riches (see for details Chapter 11, The Mystery of Wealth). Conscience must view wealth, and the pursuit of wealth, with a very wary eye. The Lord calls him a "fool" whose heart is set solely upon personal gain, and He tells a now familiar parable to illustrate the warning. A rich man tears down barns too small for his holdings. He builds bigger storehouses and says to his soul, "Soul, you have ample goods laid up for many years; take your ease, eat, drink, be merry!" "Fool! This night your soul is required of you; and the things you have prepared, whose will they be?" They will not be fruit-bearing investments for the fool. Having kept all for himself, his riches pass upon his death into the hands of others: "So is he who lays up treasure for himself, and is not rich toward God," Jesus says (Luke 12:16-21). And we know now how one becomes "rich toward

God," and that is by giving to the poor.

"How hard it will be," Jesus says, "for those who have riches to enter the kingdom of God," that is, how hard for the rich to obey God's commandments—for only they are truly citizens of a kingdom who obey its laws in obedience to its king. Indeed, the Lord goes on to say, "It is easier for a camel to go through the eye of a needle than for a rich man to enter the kingdom of God" (Mark 10:23,25).

"Come now, you rich," St. James writes, "weep and howl for the miseries that are coming upon you" (Jas. 5:1). The day of accounting is coming. Those who have made no investments beyond that judgment day do well to "weep and howl," and quickly amend their selfish ways.

Are warnings like these sounded from your pulpit? Urgently and often? Do you hear and heed them?

Or does someone try to blunt their edge by saying that salvation is only by grace?

Beware of this fatal mistake!

Of course, salvation is God's gift, out of His sheer grace—this is the teaching of the whole Bible. And grace *is* free! So the Scriptures everywhere declare. But those who have truly received this free grace at once are made investors in heaven through deeds of love: "What does it profit, my brethren, if a man says he has faith but has not works? Can his faith save him? If a brother or sister is ill-clad and in lack of daily food, and one of you says to them, 'Go in peace, be warmed and filled,' without giving them the things needed for the body, what does it profit? So faith by itself, if it has no works, is dead" (Jas. 2:14-17).

Grace, received through faith, does not ease conscience of the obligation to invest in heaven by gifts to the needy. Grace simply makes such investment possible, against the pull of self-interest and the excuses of selfishness.

What, then, shall I give the needy out of all the gifts of life, time, concern, talents, and goods which God has given me?

The Bible's answer is clear: give whatever you want to invest beyond the grave. Keep whatever you, after a few brief years, never hope to see again.

This is the clear teaching of the Scriptures, God's investment manual.

B. *PRACTICAL APPLICATION*

The church functions, by divine appointment, where the love of money and the love of God meet, and clash. Everyone is likely to feel the tensions of that conflict.

It will be pointed out, perhaps, that in fact the Bible mentions with divine approval certain very rich men. Abraham, the father of the faithful (Rom. 4:16), was rich: "Now Abram was very rich in cattle, in silver, and in gold" (Gen. 13:2). So was Joseph of Arimathea, whose riches gave him access to Pilate, the

Roman governor of Israel (Matt. 27:57-58).

And while it is true that the rich young ruler was asked to "sell all you have, and give to the poor" (Mark 10:21), it is also true that wealthy Zacchaeus was blessed upon the confession that only "the half of my goods I give to the poor" (Luke 19:8-10).

What practical instruction for conscience may be derived from these and similar Biblical examples?

We suggest these lessons:

1. The rich who win God's favor in this life, and the next, are generous to the needy. Job was rich, and received God's final blessing after many trials; he speaks for the Biblical wealthy who enjoyed God's favor: "I delivered the poor who cried, and the fatherless who had none to help him. The blessing of him who was about to perish came upon me, and I caused the widow's heart to sing for joy. I put on righteousness, and it clothed me; my justice was like a robe and a turban. I was eyes to the blind, and feet to the lame. I was a father to the poor, and I searched out the cause of him whom I did not know. I broke the fangs of the unrighteous, and made him drop his prey from his teeth" (Job 29:12-17).

2. The rich who received God's blessing in the Scriptures made double use of their wealth:

    a. They ministered directly to the needy, and

    b. They used the power entrusted them

by their God-given wealth to rescue the defenseless from the clutches of the unrighteous ("I broke the fangs of the unrighteous, and made him drop his prey from his teeth," says Job). So used, the riches kept after generous giving to the needy ("the half of my goods I give to the poor") attain the purpose for which God gives them.

3. It is not money in itself, which is a good gift from God, but the *love* of money which is evil. The aged St. Paul sums up to Timothy the verdict of his own experience in these inspired words: "For the love of money is the root of all evils; it is through this craving that some have wandered away from the faith and pierced their hearts with many pangs" (I Tim. 6:10). Paul thus repeats the teaching of our Lord in the parable of the sower: "As for what was sown among thorns, this is he who hears the word, but the cares of the world and the delight in riches choke the word, and it proves unfruitful" (Matt. 13:22). Wealth and power generously given by God to the "successful" may bear no fruit in help to the needy and upholding their cause against oppression. Why not? Because the love which should focus on the poor is turned inward to focus upon the possession of wealth and the enjoyments it seems to provide. Such love of money is condemned.

4. Joseph of Arimathea was able to ask the body of Jesus from Pontius Pilate. No doubt he found Pilate's door open to him because he was

rich. Not everyone had immediate access to Pilate's office. Wealth opens doors. What is at stake, then, is whether these doors are opened in the service of Jesus or of self. This antithesis the rich man really knows. Is his influence, for example, in local politics, or national politics, exerted for the common good or for his own? Is the influential word he might speak silenced by self-interest, or is it spoken from the rooftops for benefit of justice? God gives wealth to whom He will. Wealth not only can provide goods to supply the wants of the needy, but it is also power. The Bible does not require that every believer give all his money away. Why not? Because God has uses for the power of wealth committed to justice and right. It is the task of the Church to alert the conscience of the rich to this supreme obligation imposed by God's gifts of their wealth.

5. There remains, though, the nagging question: what, then, may anyone keep for, and spend upon, himself? The answer, which must finally be measured by each for himself, in the light of Word and of conscience as schooled by the Church is this: *I may keep and use whatever I truly need for my calling.* God allots each human a task in the world. Whatever gift is required for effectively doing that task, as in God's service, is ours for the keeping. Indeed, charity to the needy is God's way of providing them with the essentials of life requisite to their own callings. No one can decide for

another precisely what he may keep for himself. The Church through pulpit and diaconate can, and must, school conscience all it can from the Word upon this vitally important question. And God will, at the Last Day, pass judgment upon how much His gifts were in fact used in His service.

6. It is easy to understand, from our own experience, why the Bible warns so soberly, and so frequently, and so vividly against the "deceitfulness of riches." How easily we are beguiled into thinking that our wealth is all our own. That *we* have *earned* "every penny" of it. That those who have less must be lazy or spendthrift. That God signals our special virtue by giving us special blessings. All the while the Word is warning against just such self-deception.

7. In short, God's gifts of life, time, talent, possessions, skills are realized as blessings when used to sustain us in *our* callings, *and* to support the needy in *their* callings, *and* to get justice done among men to the fullest extent of our ability and power. But these gifts become a curse when exclusively ab-used for our own selfish designs.

8. "It is appointed to man once to die, and after that the judgment" (Heb. 9:27). It is with an eye upon this solemn guarantee that the church *must*, however difficult it may be, work diligently in doing what it can to alert every member to the obligations imposed upon each by whatever of God's gifts he receives. The warning given by God to the prophet Ezekiel passes on, now, to the Church, and also to everyone in the Church: "Son of man, I have made you a watchman for the house of Israel; whenever you hear a word from my mouth, you shall give them warning from me. If I say to the wicked, 'You shall surely die,' and you give him no warning, nor speak to warn the wicked from his wicked way, in order to save his life, that wicked man shall die in his iniquity; but his blood I will require at your hand. But if you warn the wicked, and he does not turn from his wickedness, or from his wicked way, he shall die in his iniquity; but you will have saved your life. Again, if a righteous man turns from his righteousness and commits iniquity, and I lay a stumbling block before him, he shall die; because you have not warned him, he shall die for his sin, and his righteous deeds which he has done shall not be remembered; but his blood I will require at your hand. Nevertheless if you warn the righteous man not to sin, and he does not sin, he shall surely live, because he took warning; and you will have saved your life" (Ezek. 3:17-21).

Stewarding is a sober business.

Pray fervently and often that God will qualify you for doing it well.

Chapter 4.

WHY GIVE AT ALL?

Why should Christians give?

The Bible clearly teaches that giving is not optional.

Why?

A. *LOVE GIVES*

Because giving is the natural expression of love. "God is love..." (I John 4:16). And, "God so loved the world that he gave his only Son..." (John 3:16). Love gives. The Son Himself equates love with giving: "Greater love has no man than this, that a man lay down (give) his life for his friends" (John 15:13). Love compels giving. Love and giving imply each other. Indeed love *is* giving. So much so that refusal to give betrays absence of love: "If any one has the world's goods and sees his brother in need, yet closes his heart to him, how does God's love abide in him?" (I John 3:17).

St. Paul defines willingness to give as evidence of love: "So give proof, before the church, of your love..." This after he has boasted of the love shown through liberality by the churches of Macedonia, "who gave according to their means, as I can testify, and beyond their means, of their own free will..." (II Cor. 8:24, 3).

Giving, then, flows from love. To love is to give. Not to give is not to love.

B. *LOVE IS MANDATORY*

"Walk in love, as Christ loved us and gave himself up for us..." (Eph. 5:2).

"And this commandment we have from him, that he who loves God should love his brother also" (I John 4:21).

"You shall love the Lord your God with all your heart, and with all your soul, and with all your mind. This is the great and first commandment. And a second is like it, You shall love your neighbor as yourself. On these two commandments depend all the law and the prophets" (Matt. 22:37-40).

Love is mandatory!

But what shall we give to God to show our love?

Obedience.

And what shall we give to our neighbors to show our love?

A generous share of the gifts God has made to us.

C. *LOVE IS THE TEST OF TRUE DISCIPLESHIP*

"By this shall all men know that you are my disciples, if you have love for one another" (John 13:35).

"This is my commandment, that you love one another as I have loved you" (John 15:12).

The true disciple loves.

The unloving lay false claim to discipleship.

D. *LOVE MEANS KEEPING THE COMMANDMENTS*

"If you love me, you will keep my commandments" (John 14:15).

"He who has my commandments and keeps them, he it is who loves me" (John 14:21). "If a man loves me, he will keep my word" (John 14:23). "For this is the love of God, that we keep his commandments" (I John 5:3).

Note very carefully: the Bible does not permit us to confuse true love with warm feelings. Emotional "love" roams around inside us. What God calls love overflows into deeds done for others, according to the commandments of God.

The confusion of feeling with love is not a minor mistake. It appears also in the substitution of "sharing faith" for sharing goods. We are quite willing to share our faith with others, something which costs us nothing. But what love requires is sharing goods which cost us a great deal of effort to obtain.

E. *THE PRESENCE OF SAVING FAITH IS CONFIRMED BY LOVE*

"For in Christ Jesus neither circumcision nor uncircumcision is of any avail, but faith working through love" (Gal. 5:6).

"If I have all faith, so as to remove mountains, but have not love, I am nothing" (I Cor. 13:2).

"For as the body apart from the spirit is dead, so faith without works is dead" (Jas. 2:26).

"God is love, and he who abides in love abides in God, and God abides in him" (I John 4:16). Because, "he who loves is born of God," while "he who does not love does not know God; for God is love" (I John 4:7-8).

True believers are obliged "to stir up one another to love and good works" (Heb. 10:24).

A saving faith is manifest in a passionate love. And such a love is manifest in good works.

F. *IN SUMMARY*

The teaching of the Scriptures is very plain:

1. To love is to give: "God so loved the world that he gave..." (John 3:16). For such evidence of love God Himself generously provides us with the gifts we are to share. He first provides what love obliges us to give.

2. Love is not optional. That is, giving and sharing are mandatory.

3. Giving thus becomes the indelible test of true discipleship.

4. But love is not warmth of feeling or fired-up emotions. Love is obedience to the commandment to share.

5. The believers's claim to saving faith is confirmed by love, that is by generous giving of all that the believer has to share.

Chapter 5.

WHY GIVE MONEY AND GOODS?

Why should giving take the form of material things?

Would it not be more "Christian" to share spiritual things? To give away my faith rather than my money? Or, is it not more obedient to support "faith ministries" than to give money to the poor, who may not merit help or are likely to squander it away? Again, is it not the sole duty of the Church to evangelize, rather than become socially activist?

These are serious questions, even if it may be suspected that they sometimes root in a preference, as noted above, for sharing faith, which cost us nothing, over sharing goods which we think were hard-earned.

The Christian preparing to answer these queries does well to recall the Lord's healing of ten lepers on the border of Samaria and Galilee. All ten had "lifted up their voices and said, 'Jesus, Master, have mercy on us'." And the Lord did. He healed them all. And then what happened? Only one paused to return thanks for his healing, and that one was a Samaritan: "Then said Jesus, 'Were there not ten cleansed? Where are the nine? Was no one found to return and give praise to God except this foreigner?' " (Luke 17:11-19).

Was the Lord unaware *before* the miracle that only one of the lepers would be grateful? Not at all. It is written of Him that, "he knew all men and needed no one to bear witness of man; for he himself knew what was in man" (John 2:25). Jesus gave healing to all ten lepers knowing full well that only one would be grateful. Lacking the endless resources of God, man must be prudent in his giving. But we must never forget that the Bible knows nothing about "the deserving poor" when it requires sharing goods with them. Rather, all who would be "sons of your Father who is in heaven" are admonished to follow His example: "for he makes his sun rise on the evil and on the good, and sends rain on the just and on the unjust" (Matt. 5:45).

The Christian gives money and goods because he is so required by the Scriptures, as the texts quoted throughout this volume abundantly demonstrate. For just such material obedience the Lord gives us the goods He expects us to share.

There is no Biblical license for substituting "sharing faith" for sharing money and material possessions. This is the burden of the prophets: "Is not this the fast that I choose: to loose the bonds of wickedness, to undo the thongs of the yoke, to let the oppressed go free, and to break every yoke? Is it not to share your bread with the hungry, and to bring the homeless poor into your house; when you see the naked, to cover him, and not to hide yourself from your own flesh?" (Is. 58:6-7). And words of the Prophet are repeated by our Lord: "Give to him who begs of you, and do not refuse him who would borrow from you" (Matt. 5:42).

The scene of the Last Judgment so vividly sketched by the Christ in Matthew 25 (vv. 31-46) makes unmistakable that evidence of love must appear in the form of very material gifts to the poor: food, drink, warmth, clothing, the touch of tender care.

True love gives in terms of need. Where the need is material, the gift must be material. Where the need is justice, the gift must be the battle to achieve that. Where the need is time, comfort, use of talent or skill, the gift must fit it.

God gives faith. He who receives faith will give generously of the goods and talents which God has given him.

CHAPTER 6.

STEWARDSHIP THROUGH THE CHURCH'S DEACONS

We never become who we ought to be completely alone.

We become who we are only in relation to others who are engaged on the same pilgrimage. This is why stewardship, which is the right use for others of God's individual gifts to each of us, is the key to our Christian life.

There is, on the one hand, individualism about human life. We are born unique individuals; we die unique individuals—no one can substitute for us, nor can we for anyone else. This was King David's lament over his wayward son Absalom: "O my son Absalom, my son, my son Absalom! Would I had died instead of you, O Absalom, my son, my son!" (II Sam. 18:33). But even God makes no provision for such a substitution. Nor can anyone act for us, or feel for us, or will for us. All our pains, joys, frustrations, fears, triumphs, failures are first of all, and inescapably, our own. So God makes us. And His judgment, finally, falls upon each of us individually: "and they were judged every man according to their works" (Rev. 20:12,13). There is no hiding in the crowd when our stewardship comes to its accounting.

Yet, on the other hand, God has so made us in His own image—that of the triune Three-in-One—that we become who we ought to be only in relation, not to ourselves, but to others. Still more, God so distributes a variety of gifts and talents among us that we are all drawn together, each to supplement his needs with the gifts alloted to others while serving the community with his own. We may speak, in this sense, of the natural family of man, a family rooting in common parents, Adam and Eve, and living in mutual service, though that harmony is sadly rent by sin.

There is another family, the new family of man, composed of those born anew through faith in Jesus Christ. This family constitutes the Church. So closely does their mutual stewardship, in love, unite true believers in Christ that their union in the Church is referred to as Christ's Body: "so we, though many, are one body in Christ, and individually members one of another" (Rom. 12:5). The common term "Church member" gains special significance from the truth revealed here. We are not "members" by virtue of belonging, as one may belong to a club. We are "members one of another" because the Church to which we affirm allegiance is a **body**! This means that through stewardship we serve each other as members of a body do.

But, sharing as the Church still does in the universal fallenness of man, her fundamental oneness emerges in history as a variety of institutional forms, sometimes at odds with one another. The new has not completely eclipsed the old.

The Church as Body becomes most concretely visible in the local congregation, whatever its denominational affiliation. Here the Body meets at appointed times, listens to instruction through its ministry from the Word of the Lord, worships through the sacraments, and unites for praise and prayer.

As a genuine Body, the local congregation is also obliged to render true stewardship of the Lord's gifts to members of the Body as individuals. The congregation exercises such stewardship through the office of those commonly called deacons, and collectively the diaconate.

Here, as in Chapter 14 below, we take special note of diaconal stewardship, done in the name of the congregation—discussed in greater detail in our **Deacons Handbook** to which this volume is closely related.

Turn briefly, then, to your stewardship of God's goods as exercised through a diaconate.

Let it be said very plainly, and at once: a body without hands, or eyes and ears, is not wholly a body.

Deacons are seeing eyes, hearing ears, and serving hands of the congregation, that is, of any congregation which is determined to be a true manifestation of the *Body* of Jesus Christ. The presence and activity of the diaconate declares to the congregation, and to the community: here *is* the visible, concrete, unmistakable Body of the Lord, redeemed by Him for good works (Eph. 2:10)!

This, then is the summary answer to the question: why give to, and through, the Church? To demonstrate that you are, and know that you are, member of a Body—and that a body lacking hands, or hands lacking gifts, is less than the Lord's Body is called to be.

The Church, visible in each local congregation, is the Body through which the Lord Jesus Christ chooses to act in your community. And the diaconate is that Body's hands outstretched to serve, that Body's eyes alert to signs of distress, and that Body's ears ever open to even the silent cries of despair.

As the Lord's Body, the Church provides Him with lips to proclaim His Word, thus bearing courageous witness to His Truth through her pulpit ministry. As the Lord's Body, the Church provides Him with seeing eye and hearing ear and serving hand through the diaconate. And as the Lord's Body, the Church elects an eldership to oversee obedience to His will (see our *Elders Handbook*).

All this was self-evident to the New Testament Church, but because ours is an era of individualism, of doing one's own thing in one's own way, deacons must be fully prepared to answer the query: why should I give through you?

To that end, we offer the following perspectives:

A. *PRACTICAL PERSPECTIVE*

1. From a purely business point of view, the diaconate assures the congregation of a systematic, disciplined, orderly approach to meeting the overall financial and material necessities requisite to its existence and function.

2. An active diaconate assures the congregation that each individual member's material and financial needs, even when unknown to most others, are systematically discovered and met. This is important because:

a. Very real needs could be otherwise overlooked, especially when these are hidden behind a facade of, "Oh, everything's fine."

b. The diaconate brings together resources—in money and in talent—which individual members of the Body could not always provide, nor so well focus.

c. The diaconate remembers routine services, perhaps on schedule week after week, which individual members might well neglect.

d. Knowledge of the active presence of a

diaconate relieves the conscience of individual members who wonder, otherwise, if there be needy and if their wants are being supplied—and who quite honestly confess that if such services depended upon themselves, many needs would go unnoticed or unmet.

e. Each member knows that his own contribution, however small, becomes a part of the whole program of diakonia. *Each* thus shares in the service of *all* who need service. Through her deacons, in short, the congregation does indeed act...like a Body!

3. In a practical way, too, the pulpit ministry can hardly lay on the conscience of the individual what the congregation as a Body neglects to pursue, namely the relief of the needy. Diaconal services do not entirely supplant individual charity. Rather they model it, and involve the skills and talents of the whole for the benefit of those who can use them. There will be good works of all kinds left to do for those who have an eye and ear for wanting to do them.

4. Practically, too, congregational diakonia has virtually no overhead. Neither deacons nor members accept reward for their services—this side of the grave. The church building provides most of the facilities. The full value of each gift, therefore, makes its way to the recipients. This is less likely to be true of charities set up independently of the Church and run as private ventures, however well-intentioned. The dia-

conal dollar, or gift in kind, or focusing of skill or talent, is carefully stewarded charity.

B. *WITNESS PERSPECTIVE*

Diaconal service is the Lord's prescribed form of witness: "Let your light so shine before men, that they may see your good works and give glory to your Father who is in heaven" (Matt. 5:16). St. Paul advises the Church to be "children of God without blemish in the midst of a crooked and perverse generation, among whom you shine as lights in the world..." (Phil. 2:15). And St. Peter writes: "Maintain good conduct among the Gentiles, so that in case they speak against you as wrongdoers, they may see your good deeds and glorify God on the day of visitation" (I Pet. 2:12).

Consider, from this perspective:

1. Diaconal service boosts, as it were, the Church to a hilltop position. The Lord declares that, "A city set on a hill cannot be hid." How, then, does the Church become visible? This we have already noticed: by diaconal good works, which glorify the Lord's Father in heaven. These are the deeds which testify that the congregation has heard and understands, as a Body, her Lord's instruction: "Not everyone who says to me, 'Lord, Lord,' will enter the kingdom of heaven, but he who does the will of my Father who is in heaven" (Matt. 7:21).

2. Diaconal service bears evangelical witness to the world by displaying the fruits of

faith: "So, every sound tree bears good fruit," and "By their fruits will they be known" (Matt. 7:17, 16).

3. Diaconal service bears witness to the congregation itself that she has heard and understands her Lord's commands, and dwells, therefore, in the warmth of His love: "If you keep my commandments, you will abide in my love, just as I have kept my Father's commandments and abide in his love" (John 15:10). And, indeed, a congregation that serves unitedly through the diaconate grows into more virile unity in the process. Muscles used grow stronger.

4. Diaconal good works bear witness to the congregation's awareness that here is a very special and unique form of unity, that of a Body whose hands are busy through an office instituted by God for just this purpose.

5. The Body's deed witness is correlative to its pulpit's word witness. The Bible nowhere suggests that either one may be substituted for the other. The Word witnesses to the Truth that self-sacrifice lies at the heart of Christianity. The deed, done by the Body and for the Body through the diaconate, as well as individually, witnesses to the fact that the Word has been heard and believed. Both forms of witness speak for the Lord to the world.

C. *THEOLOGICAL PERSPECTIVE*

There are theological perspectives on giving

through the diaconate, like these:

1. The office of the deacon is the New Testament form of the Old Testament office of the Levite. St. Paul carefully specifies divinely inspired requirements for deacons (I Tim. 3:8-13). Sectarians may neglect the diaconate, but a Church which has no deacons lacks one of the essentials of her being.

2. The deacon replaces the so-called "Christian communism" practiced by the fledgling Church. This is sometimes overlooked by liberation theologians. The early enthusiasm reflected by the initial believers' "having all things in common" quickly broke down. The "Hellenists" (Greek speaking believers, perhaps immigrant Jews) murmured that "their widows were neglected in the daily distribution" from the common fund (Acts 6:1), showing that the communal sharing reported earlier (Acts 2:44, and 4:32) lapsed early. And the diaconate, not a holding all things in common, soon becomes the normative model provided to the Church by the New Testament. Deacons, not communism, respond to needs within—and without—the Body. The office of deacon declares that systematic diakonia, rather than enforced Communist equality, is the Church's inspired answer to disparities in wealth and talent. This, in our times especially, is a fundamental theological lesson for the Church—and the deacons in particular—to learn and remember, and practice.

3. The diaconate is the Protestant substitute for the Catholic religious order. Through the deacons, as well as by using skills along-beside them, the Church member shares of his gifts in talent and goods with the needy.

4. Giving through the diaconate avoids all ostentation, and is thus obedient to the Lord's command: "Thus, when you give alms, sound no trumpet before you, as the hypocrites do in the synagogues and in the streets, that they may be praised by men. Truly, I say to you, they have their reward. But when you give alms, do not let your left hand know what your right hand is doing, so that your alms may be in secret; and your Father who sees in secret will reward you" (Matt. 6:2-4). Through the deacons, the largest gift merges with the smallest, exactly as the Head of the Body requires. God knows. That is enough.

5. It may well be that those who are surprised, on the Judgment Day, by the extent of their service to the needy, in fact performed that service through the deacons: "'Lord, when did we see thee hungry and feed thee, or thirsty and give thee drink? And when did we see thee a stranger and welcome thee, or naked and clothe thee? And when did we see thee sick or in prison and visit thee?'" (Matt. 25:37-39). A striking surprise awaits those who serve through the Body by her deacons.

6. St. Paul teaches explicitly that God deliberately distributes gifts in difference and variety so that members of the Body (and of the human race) will be drawn to each other by need of each other's goods and talents (I Cor. 12, the whole chapter). This mutual sharing by divine design is facilitated in and for the Church by an alert and active diaconate.

D. *CONCLUSION*

The import, we believe, of all the above is clear: the diaconate is a key office in the Church. Giving to, and through the deacons is primary giving, first-claim giving, not grudging or after-thought charity. Just as membership in the Lord's Body has a basic priority in all of life, so sharing by way of the Body's hands has a basic priority in congregational membership. The priestly office of each believer, like the priestly office of Christ, is fulfilled in self-sacrificial devotion to the internal and external needs of the Church and her parish.

Chapter 7.

HOW MUCH? (FROM MITES TO MILLIONS)

Has the Church no Word from the Lord as to exactly how much the believer owes God? That is to say, owes the Church as representative of God?

Yes, it has that.

The believer, because he is a true believer, knows very well that he owes God everything: "...for the world and all that is in it is mine" (Ps. 50:12). God has first claim by right of ownership to everything each of us calls his own.

To ask with the Psalmist, "What shall I render to the Lord for all his bounty to me?" (Ps. 116:12) can only be completely answered by the acknowledgment: all, Lord, is thine!

Moreover, God gives in order that His obedient children may give: "And God is able to provide you with every blessing in abundance, so that you may always have enough of everything and may provide in abundance for every good work" (II Cor. 9:8).

Can we come no closer than this to some

measure of "how much" we owe the Lord?

The most ancient measure of what the believer owes to God is the tithe, one-tenth of what God gives to us. The Israelites were obliged to give the Levites one-tenth of the produce of their soil, of their orchards, of their flocks. And every third year a tithe—probably a second tithe—was to be shared with the stranger and the poor (Lev. 27:30-33; Deut. 12:5-18).

In addition, the Lord required "offerings" of His people, of two basic types: 1) offerings for sin, and 2) thank offerings. The prophet Malachi charges Israel with robbing God by neglecting both tithes *and* offerings: "Will man rob God? Yet you are robbing me. But you say, 'How are we robbing thee?' In your tithes and offerings. You are cursed with a curse, for you are robbing me; the whole nation of you. Bring the full tithes into the storehouse, that there may be food in my house; and thereby put me to the test, says the Lord of hosts, if I will not open the windows of heaven for you and pour down for you an overflowing blessing" (Mal. 3:8-10).

There is no suggestion in the Scriptures that the Lord's demand upon the Old Testament Church is abated for the New. Nor is there any suggestion that what we give elsewhere can be "credited," so to speak, against the tithe owed the Church. Indeed, St. Paul sets a higher standard, it may well be, especially for those who are richly blessed: "Upon the first day of the week let every one of you lay by him in store, as God hath prospered him..." (I Cor. 16:2). The more generous God, the more generous we!

Is God pleased, then with our liberality? Indeed: "...for God loves a cheerful giver" (II Cor. 9:7).

There is, however, one more thing to be added on the matter of "how much" do we owe the Lord and His Church?

It is taught us by the familiar story recounted in both St. Mark and St. Luke: "And he sat down opposite the (temple) treasury, and watched the multitude putting money into the treasury. Many rich people put in large sums. And a poor widow came, and put in two copper coins, which make a penny. And he called his disciples to him, and said to them, 'Truly, I say to you, this poor widow has put in more than all those who are contributing to the treasury. For they all contributed out of their abundance; but she out of her poverty has put in everything she had, her whole living' " (Mark 12:41-44; Luke 21:1-4).

By making such a point of calling His disciples, who represent the Church, to Him, the Lord intends that we should take careful note of what He has to say. And what does He have to say?

It is this: God measures the amount of what we give by comparison with the amount we keep for ourselves. The widow gave most because she kept back nothing. The others gave less because they kept back more.

This is not pleasant truth to hear. Especially not for those who think themselves very generous because their gifts are substantial, and who expect that the Church and the Lord will think the same.

There must be no mistake about this: the Lord does love the cheerful giver. The Lord does expect those whom He has richly blessed to be richly generous. And the Lord does accept each gift as investment in heaven. All this is true. Let those who are generous always be appreciated.

But when we are asking "how much" do I owe the Lord's work in the Church and for the neighbor, then we come finally to the Lord's own measure of how much it is that we really give, say in comparison with one another. And then His teaching is clear: he gives most, in the sight of heaven, who keeps back least by comparison. He gives least, in the sight of heaven, who keeps back most by comparison.

This follows, when we come to think about it, from the fact that all we have is God's to begin with. What we give, He gave us to share; what we keep is still His, not shared.

The King James Version speaks of the poor widow's gift as "two mites," the smallest Hebrew coins. From mites to millions may loom differently in the sight of God than in ours—and the giver's!

Remember, too, that the Bible takes very seriously a dividing-line we tend to ignore, namely the dividing-line marked by death. In terms of giving, death marks the watershed of reward. Generosity which is publicly acknowledged this side of the grave already has its reward. Generosity done without fanfare this side of the grave is rewarded in heaven: "Thus, when you give alms, sound no trumpet before you, as the hypocrites do in the synagogues and in the streets, that they may be praised by men. Truly, I say to you, they have their reward. But when you give alms, do not let your left hand know what your right hand is doing, so that your alms may be in secret; and your Father who sees in secret will reward you" (Matt. 6:2-4). When God comes in judgment, on the Last Day, He will reward: "Behold, the Lord God comes with might, and his arm rules for him; behold, his reward is with him, and his recompense before him" (Is. 40:10).

For this reason the Apostle can say, "And let us not grow weary in well-doing, for in due season we shall reap, if we do not lose heart" (Gal. 6:9).

In times of discouragement, let Christians take heart from the knowledge that quietly and all about us good stewardship is being done, seen now by the untiring eye of God to be rewarded when it is no longer *today:* "For truly I say to you, whoever gives you a cup of water to drink because you bear the name of Christ, will by no means lose His reward" (Mark 9:41). Reward-bearing service is out of the reach of no one. But reward-seeking notoriety risks having all the praise it will receive from men rather than from God.

The Lord's warning is unmistakable: "Beware of practicing your piety before men in order to be seen by them; for then you will have no reward from your Father who is in heaven" (Matt. 6:1).

One thing more:

Tithing as a measure of good stewardship does not only apply to money and goods. It applies no less to time, talent, skills, and personal services of all kinds.

Where money or goods will meet a need, then money or goods the steward must, if he can, provide. But the common criticism of the welfare system that it tries to solve all problems by "throwing money at them" applies no less to good stewarding. There are things that money can't buy, like genuine friendship, persistent compassion, the thoughtful word or call, the affirming glance or warming smile. These, too, fall under the claim of the Lord upon a tithe of our capacities. And, happily, these are within the reach of everyone who remembers to share them. Life itself, in all of the forms it can take, is ours to steward—for years three-score and ten, if the Lord wills. Consider every good that you can do for another a part of the tithe claimed by the Lord. And remember that He speaks not only of tithes but also, and in addition, of that second mile, the offerings.

Chapter 8.

SACRIFICE AND STEWARDSHIP

Christians are described in Scripture as "a royal priesthood" (I Pet. 2:9). The Apostle picks up here God's description of His people Israel: "and you shall be to me a kingdom of priests and a holy nation" (Ex. 19:6).

What does it mean that true believers are priests, and belong to a royal priesthood?

It means that the Christian, as king so rules over himself that, as priest, he sacrifices his own self-interests to those of others. This is a royal priesthood!

A. *SACRIFICE*

Sacrifice is at the very heart of Christianity.

The vicarious self-sacrifice of Jesus Christ on Calvary highlights the fact that sacrifice is of the essence of our religion.

The believer does not avoid sacrifice through faith in Jesus. It is a true and living faith that makes the believer's priestly self-sacrifice possible. True Christians are, as the Bible declares, "a royal priesthood". That is to say, true Christians are good stewards.

What is sacrifice?

A little child disobeys his mother. He goes out and picks a wild flower to bring her. Why? Partly because he hopes that thus he will appease her annoyance and lighten his probable punishment. But more fundamentally he wants to get "right" with his mother again by making an "offering" that will erase the wrong that separates them and troubles his conscience. Sacrifice is like that. It is an "offering" given to higher authority to undo the effects of disobedience, to make things "right" again.

Sacrifice reaches far back into the history of Christianity and of other forms of religion. We deal here only with sacrifice in Christianity, where it is fundamental.

We know that God created man good and in His own Image (Gen. 1:26-27), and that man breaks the divine law and thus alienates himself and his descendents from his Creator (Gen. 3:1-20).

Estranged from God, as a disobedient child is estranged from his mother, man early turns to sacrifice. Cain and Abel, first sons of Adam and Eve, bring their offerings to God (Gen. 4:3-4). Noah sacrifices to God after escape from the flood (Gen. 18:20). Abraham (whose name was at first Abram) builds an altar to commemorate God's promise to him of the land of Canaan for his descendents (Gen. 15:7).

When the Lord liberates Israel from slavery in Egypt, He lays down rules which make sacrifice the heart of worship. And He requires that the Levites, descendents of Jacob's third son Levi, shall be servants of the altar and in the temple later built around it. The tribe of Levi inherits no land in Canaan. So unique is their service to God and His people that they live off the gifts which are presented by other tribes to the Lord: "Therefore Levi has no portion or inheritance with is brothers; the Lord is his inheritance, as the Lord your God said to him" (Deut. 10:9).

What service do the Levites perform?

Theirs is a dual service: 1) Aaron, the brother to Moses, and all his descendents are priests. They serve at the altar, making sacrifice of the peoples' gifts to the Lord. 2) All other descendents of Levi are called Levites, and their service is to prepare the peoples' gifts for sacrifice, and to care for all tasks involving the temple. We commonly read, therefore, of "the priests and Levites" as occupying offices in the temple.

For a detailed outline of Israel's sacrificial system, the reader can consult a Bible dictionary. What concerns us here is that the temple sacrifices were of two basic kinds: 1) offerings made for sin, and 2) offerings made in thanksgiving, both for forgiveness of sins and for God's many other blessings.

B. *MEANING OF SACRIFICE*

What was the meaning of the sacrificial system imposed by God upon Israel?

The priests offered the peoples' sacrifices upon the altar. In so doing they foreshadow Christ's sacrifice of Himself upon the altar of Calvary. As the New Testament epistle to the Hebrews makes clear, the temple sacrifices come to their culmination, and conclusion, in the death of Jesus upon the cross. The work of the priests and Levites comes to fulfillment. The altar of the Old Testament Church then becomes the table of the Lord's Supper in the New Testament Church.

The sacrificial system has found its meaning, and the symbol of the altar has given way to the symbol of the table—though in essence both imply the same thing: sacrifice.

C. *ENTER THE STEWARD*

It is a striking thing that the deacon first appears in the New Testament Church as waiting on tables! The account is familiar: "Now in these days when the disciples were increasing in number, the Hellenists murmured against the Hebrews because their widows were neglected in the daily distribution. And the twelve summoned the body of the disciples and said, 'It is not right that we should give up preaching the word of the Lord to serve tables. Therefore, brethren, pick out from among you seven men of good repute, full of the Spirit and of wisdom, whom we may appoint to this duty. But we will devote ourselves to prayer and to the ministry of the word' '' (Acts 6:1-4).

Is it just a coincidence that the office of deacon arises in connection with table service—though it will soon expand to other forms of charity, and that our stewardship is modeled by serving tables?

Not at all! Nothing in the history of the Church is mere coincidence.

Three tables all point to the same thing: the table called "altar" in the Old Testament; the table of the Lord's Supper; and the tables served by deacons—all three relate to sacrifice, which remains at the heart of Christianity.

This becomes evident through a further brief look back into the Old Testament Church.

D. *FROM LEVITE TO PRIESTHOOD OF ALL BELIEVERS*

Old Testament sacrifices consisted of animals, birds, firstfruits of the harvest. These were things. Things which, indeed, the giver might have used for himself. Sacrifice implies, then, self-sacrifice, too. The giver surrenders to the Lord, and to the temple, what he could have made use of. This is the first step in sacrifice: give to God what you could use for yourself.

But this is only the first step. What God sees is the heart of the giver. Does the sin-offering reflect a heart truly repentant, truly determined to amend its ways? This is what genuine sacrifice for sin required. Sacrifice is the outward symbol of an inward state; and if the heart is not true, the sacrifice is not acceptable to God. He makes this clear, again and again, through His prophets: "Has the Lord as great delight in burnt offerings and sacrifices, as in obeying the voice of the Lord? Behold, to obey is better than sacrifice, and to hearken than the fat of rams" (I Sam. 15:22). This is the Word of the Lord to Saul, first king of Israel, spoken by Samuel the Lord's prophet.

To those whose heart was not in accord with their offerings, the Lord declares: "Bring no more vain offerings; incense is an abomination to me...When you spread forth your hands, I will hide my eyes from you; even though you make many prayers, I will not listen; your hands are full of blood" (Is. 1:13, 15).

And how, then does sacrifice become acceptable?

The Lords answers: "Wash yourselves; make yourselves clean; remove the evil of your doings from before my eyes; cease to do evil, learn to do good; seek justice, correct oppression; defend the fatherless, plead for the widow" (Is. 1:15-17). Again: "Is not this the fast that I choose: to loose the bonds of wickedness, to undo the thongs of the yoke, to let the oppressed go free, and to break every yoke? Is it not to share your bread with the hungry, and bring the homeless poor into your house; when you see the naked, to cover him; and not to hide yourself from your own flesh?'' (Is. 58:6-7).

The temple sacrifices must represent willing *self*-sacrifice for others, or the temple sacrifices are unacceptable. The believer must love God above all (Deut. 6:5) and show it by loving his neighbor as himself (Lev. 19:18). This is the meaning of the sacrificial system.

But where will the believer find the strength to deny self-interest and practice self-sacrifice? How can the believer obey the command, ''Wash yourselves; make yourselves clean''? Is not this just what sacrifice was supposed to do? How, then, come to sacrifice with already clean hands?

We must recall, here, that Old Testament sacrifice was of two kinds: 1) for sin, and 2) in thanksgiving. The first provided clean hands for the second. The sacrifice of thanksgiving could not reach God unless it rose out of a heart cleansed of sin and thus liberated to obedience. Still more, the sacrifice of thanksgiving was acceptable to God only if it reflected the will to a life of obedience as required by God—this is the burden of the prophets, as we have observed. Not the life of perfection, for then the sacrifice for sin would no longer be necessary. But the life striving for perfection, through obedience to divine law.

But the temple sacrifices for sin only symbolized the true sacrifice for sin—Christ's self-sacrifice on the altar of Calvary. When that happened, the table of the Lord took the place of the altar, and the Old Testament Levitical office had run its course. The ministry to the altar ended. And re-appeared in a new ministry to another table: the ministry of all believers aided by the deacon.

The New Testament congregation gathers, now, around the new "altar" of the Lord's table as He commanded (Matt. 26:26-28; I Cor. 11:23-26). There the believer is once again confirmed in his liberation from sin and selfishness. He is once more stimulated to self-sacrifice through the gift of goods, time, talent to the Lord.

And, turning from the Lord's table, how shall the thankful Church deliver her gifts to the Lord?

Obviously, in two parallel ways: 1) by everyone's sacrificial sharing, as believer-priests, time, talent, goods, and money with those in need of them, and 2) by funneling through the Church's appointed ministry of mercy, the diaconate, whatever is better given that way.

As the Old Testament believer laid his gifts upon the altar, so the New Testament believer lays his gifts upon the table—for distribution to the needy via the diaconate; and, as New Testament priest stewards his goods for the needs of others.

What could be more appropriate?

The service required by God of Israel was

symbolized in the temple sacrifice, representing self-sacrifice for the neighbor. Ministering to this sacrifice were the Levites.

The service required by God of the New Israel, the New Testament Church, is in the temples where God now chooses to be found and worshipped—the persons of the neighbor. Ministering to this sacrifice are the Body of believers, individually, and collectively through their diaconates.

Thus the writer to the Hebrews first explains the transition from the Old Testament service to the New Testament Gospel, and then relates this to the believer's response: "Do not neglect to do good and to share what you have, for such sacrifices are pleasing to God" (Heb. 13:16).

It now becomes clear why all believers are described in the Scriptures (both Old and New Testaments) as being themselves "priests".

God says to Israel, through Moses: "...you shall be to me a kingdom of priests and a holy nation" (Ex. 19:6). St. Peter writes: "Come to him, that living stone, rejected by men but in God's sight chosen and precious; and like living stones be yourselves built into a spiritual house, to be a holy priesthood, to offer spiritual sacrifices acceptable to God through Jesus Christ" (I Pet. 2:4-5). And St. John writes in Revelation: "To him, who loves us and has freed us from our sins by his blood and made us a kingdom, priests to his God and

Father, to him be glory and dominion for ever and ever. Amen" (Rev. 1:5-6).

The believer as priest presides at the daily sacrifice of his own selfishness, and gives the fruits of such self-sacrifice to God: "I appeal to you therefore, brethren, by the mercies of God, to present your bodies as a living sacrifice, holy and acceptable to God, which is your spiritual worship" (Rom. 12:1). Such sacrifice can range from the smallest act of self-denial, done in obedience to divine command, through the sharing of goods, talents, time, energies with others, to the very sacrifice of life itself: "Greater love has no man than this, that a man lay down his life for his friends" (John 15:13).

Thus does the divine plan come full circle: from the fore-shadowing of Calvary in the Old Testament priesthood and Levites, through the liberating reality of Christ's own fulfillment of the promise, to the believer's thankful response in the priestly sacrifice of himself for the good of others.

In short, Christians, be good stewards!

Chapter 9.

LEVELS OF AWARENESS: FAITH AND WORKS

You as believer will be, right now, at some level in understanding the relationship between faith and good works as that applies to your exercise of Christian stewardship. We see these levels as follows:

A. *LEVEL ONE: ARE YOU SAVED?*

At this stage all emphasis falls upon salvation by faith. No necessary relation is perceived between salvation and service.

The Bible knows this level: "For by grace you have been saved through faith; and this is not your own doing, it is the gift of God—not because of works, lest any man should boast" (Eph. 2:8-9). Assurance of salvation exists, at this stage, by itself. If the believer thinks at all in terms of charity to the needy, it is as something added to salvation. The believer's focus is far more on sharing the faith, and supporting the congregation for this purpose, than on sustaining a diaconate for service to the poor.

Congregational offerings are taken for evangelism. Acts of charity are thought largely to be the responsibility of the individual believer as the Spirit moves him. Theologically, stress falls upon grace as opposed to law, on the New Testament in contrast to the Old. Talk of good works is likely to be interpreted as "the social gospel," or as a futile effort to gain heaven by one's own exertions.

At this stage self-sacrificial stewardship seems largely optional.

B. *LEVEL TWO: VOLUNTARY GRATITUDE*

The believer is indeed saved by grace. This fundamental truth the Bible repeats over and over: "Since all have sinned and fall short of the glory of God, they are justified by grace as a gift, through the redemption which is in Christ Jesus" (Rom. 3:24). "As far as the east is from the west, so far does He remove our transgressions from us" (Ps. 103:12).

Thinking on such unmerited salvation, believers find themselves stirred to gratitude. Moreover, they are aware that gratitude must be more than lip-service. Does not the Prophet Isaiah condemn those "who draw near with their mouth and honor me with their lips, while their hearts are far from me" (Is. 29:13)? A judgment reinforced by the Lord Himself (Matt. 15:8-9). Much of the congregation's effort to give material expression to their gratitude may still go into support of word-evangelism, both that of the congregation itself and that of radio and television crusadists.

But gratitude may also take the form of charity.

Stewardship has moved from the optional to the desirable.

C. *LEVEL THREE: MANDATORY GRATITUDE*

Reading on in Paul's letter to the Ephesians, just past the point quoted under Level One above, the believer is told: "For we are His workmanship, created in Christ Jesus for good works, which God prepared beforehand, that we should walk in them" (Eph. 2:10).

We are not saved *by* good works, true indeed, but we are saved *for* doing them, no doubt about that! Reflecting upon the import of this and similar Biblical teaching, Christians move into two new awarenesses:

1. Salvation is *both* individual and communal. Faith unites believers both to Jesus Christ and to His Body, the Church. Each is a *member*, that is a living part, of the whole congregation. St. Paul graphically describes what such membership in the Lord's Body, which is the Church, means in the twelfth chapter of First Corinthians. Paul says, for example, that God distributes various gifts to members of the Church so that, by mutual service and dependence, the Body is drawn the closer together: "...that the members may have the same care for one another. If one member

suffers, all suffer together; if one member is honored, all rejoice together" (I Cor. 12:25-26). Again: "Now there are varieties of gifts, but the same Spirit; and there are varieties of service, but the same Lord; and there are varieties of working, but it is the same God who inspires them all in every one" (I Cor. 12:4-6).

2. Believers become aware that in their mutual concern for each other, the members of the Body present a powerful witness to the world: "Maintain good conduct among the Gentiles, so that in case they speak against you as wrongdoers, they may see your good deeds and glorify God..." (I Pet. 2:12). The congregation finds itself, as it were, set upon a hill, in thus being concerned for each other, and rejoice in the reminder: "Let your light so shine before men, that they may see your good works and give glory to your Father who is in heaven" (Matt. 5:16).

At this stage stewardship is recognized as necessary.

D. *LEVEL FOUR: FAITH IS GOOD WORKS*

The Lord asks: "Who are my mother and my brothers?" And He answers: "Whoever does the will of God is my brother, and sister, and mother" (Mark 3:33, 35).

At this stage in Christian awareness it is perceived that faith and behavior merge. We are no longer able to separate salvation by faith from the doing of good works through faith in obedience to the will (that is, law) of God. The desire to do good, in gratitude for salvation, is now seen not simply as evidence of rebirth in Christ Jesus, it *is* rebirth in Christ Jesus. Doing good is the other face of being saved—for it is to do good that we are saved! Or, better, we enter upon salvation through obedience which is displayed in good works. This is evident throughout the Scriptures:

1. To believe in Jesus as Savior is to obey Christ as Lord: "And by this we may be sure that we know him, if we keep His commandments" (I John 2:3). Again: "If you love me, you will keep my commandments" (John 14:15). And once more: "Not every one who says to me, 'Lord, Lord,' shall enter the kingdom of heaven, but he who does the will of my Father who is in heaven" (Matt. 7:21). Those who believe obey, and those who obey believe.

2. Being wise unto salvation means building upon the Rock, which is Christ. But such building consists in doing the good works which Christ the Rock commands: "Every one then who hears these words of mine and does them will be like a wise man who built his house upon the rock; and the rain fell, and the floods came, and the winds blew and beat upon that house, but it did not fall, because it had been founded on the rock" (Matt. 7:24-25). "Be doers of the word, and not hearers only, deceiving yourselves...he who looks into the

perfect law, the law of liberty, and perseveres, being no hearer that forgets but a doer that acts, he shall be blessed in his doing'' (Jas. 1:22, 25).

3. To know God is to do justice: "Did not your father eat and drink and do justice and righteousness? Then it was well with him. He judged the cause of the poor and needy; then it was well. Is not this to know me? says the Lord'' (Jer. 22:15-16). "Is not this the fast that I choose: to loose the bonds of wickedness, to undo the thongs of the yoke, to let the oppressed go free, and to break every yoke? Is it not to share your bread with the hungry, and bring the homeless poor into your house; when you see the naked, to cover him, and not to hide yourself from your own flesh? Then shall your light break forth like the dawn..." (Is. 58:6-8). Again, the Prophet declares: "They shall not hurt or destroy in all my holy mountain..." Why not? "For the earth will be full of the knowledge of the Lord as the waters cover the sea'' (Is. 11:9). The knowledge of God *is* the doing of right, that is, the doing of His will.

4. The believer is required to love: "Owe no one anything, except to love one another; for he who loves his neighbor has fulfilled the law'' (Rom. 13:8). Again: "For the whole law is fulfilled in one word, 'You shall love your neighbor as yourself''' (Gal. 5:14). And the Lord adds this: "By this all men will know that you are my disciples, if you have love for one another'' (John 13:35).

At this stage of awareness, stewardship is perceived as registering the spiritual temperature of the believer. Good works witness to the warmth of love in the Body and to the world much as a thermometer registers warmth of weather.

Here priestly self-sacrifice is recognized as being indispensable.

E. *TO ATTAIN LEVEL FOUR*

Obviously, level four awareness must be the believer's goal. Can this level be sought—and found? Is so, how will you go about that?

Begin with the knowledge that the life of love is not natural to us. By nature, we are ruled by self-interest. The Lord requires a life of self-sacrifice. The gradual substitution of the will to self-sacrifice for the will to self-interest is what progress in the Christian life consists of. The goal of the Church herself is promotion of the life of love in each member of the congregation. And the congregation's united progress toward this goal will be measured on its diaconal thermometer.

How does the Church, then, go about seeking level four awareness?

1. By the preaching of the Word: "So faith comes from what is heard, and what is heard comes by the preaching of Christ" (Rom. 10:17). Faith matures more and more into the life of love under persistent preaching of the

Scriptures: "All scripture is inspired by God and profitable for teaching, for reproof, for correction, and for training in righteousness, that the man of God may be complete, equipped for every good work" (II Tim. 3:16-17). Preaching is always the key, and the congregation set on a hill by the witness of its good works is evidently the place where the Word of God is most effectively preached.

2. Those who ardently desire developing the gift of faith can seek diligently to do the works of faith. The Bible clearly specifies what works a true faith leads the believer to do: "...the fruit of the Spirit is love, joy, peace, patience, kindness, goodness, faithfulness, gentleness, self-control...." (Gal. 5:22-23). "Love is patient and kind; love is not jealous or boastful; it is not arrogant or rude. Love does not insist on its own way; it is not irritable or resentful; it does not rejoice at wrong, but rejoices in the right. Love bears all things, believes all things, hopes all things, endures all things" (I Cor. 13:4-7). An effort to live such a life of love opens the heart to greater possession by faith.

Again and again, the Old Testament prophets and Christ Himself stress the fact that a hard heart presents a deaf ear to the Word. And the heart is hardened by persistent refusal to support the needy and to do good works among men. All who seek to open their hearts to the Spirit and the Word can prepare the soil in which faith finds fruit by doing the works of faith, and through presenting themselves where the Word is truly preached.

F. *IN SUMMARY*

Christian stewardship is not an accidental, optional, perhaps haphazard series of handouts given by Christians and the Church on their way to glory. Good personal stewardship, also flowering in diaconal service, *is* the way to glory, and the more certainly the congregation is on its way to heaven the more certainly will its *works* testify to the love of God.

Chapter 10.

GOD AND CONSCIENCE

A. INVESTMENT AND RETURN

1. *God and Free Enterprise*

The Lord God is a free enterpriser. This is one reason why Karl Marx, who was not a free enterpriser, rejected God.

God is a free enterpriser because He expects a return on His investments. Jesus' parables of the talents (Matt. 25:14-30) and of the pounds (Luke 19:11-27) clearly teach us that God expects interest on the talents He invests in each of us. This is implied in the Lord's command: "You, therefore, must be perfect..." (Matt. 5:48).

In short, all of God's gifts to mankind are as a divine investment upon which the Investor expects full return. And we know from the whole tenor of the Scriptures what the nature of that return should be: so putting our talents at God's disposal that others derive benefit from the gifts given to us. This is summarized in the Golden Rule: "And as you wish that men would do to you, so do to them" (Luke 6:31).

This ideal order of return on divine investment is shattered by sin. Paul vividly describes it: "...they exchanged the truth about God for a lie and worshipped and served the creature rather than the Creator, who is blessed forever! Amen" (Rom. 1:25). Paul goes on to detail the consequences of this substitution of the lie for the truth: "They were filled with all manner of wickedness, evil, covetousness, malice. Full of envy, murder, strife, deceit, malignity, they are gossips, slanderers, haters of God, insolent, haughty, boastful, inventors of evil, disobedient to parents, foolish, faithless, heartless, ruthless. Though they know God's decree that those who do such things deserve to die, they not only do them but approve those who practice them" (Rom. 1:29-32).

The divine Investor is willfully defrauded of His return. At the heart of this theft is false worship. Men bow before their own lusts instead of before their Creator, because they are in bondage to the Devil, author of the lie!

2. *Out of Egypt*

Israel's bondage in Egypt symbolizes mankind's bondage to sin and Satan. The Lord's liberation of Israel from Egyptian bondage symbolizes His liberation of all true believers from bondage to self-interest and

Satan, through the self-sacrificial death of Jesus Christ. On Jesus the Lord laid "the iniquity of us all" (Is. 53:6), so that by faith the believer is "free from the law of sin and death" (Rom. 8:2).

What, then, is this "by faith" which frees us from Egyptian bondage? It is the gift of God which sets us once more in the position of returning God some interest on His investment in us. Our gifts and talents are liberated from bondage to self-lust, and freed for service to others in the name of God. To all those liberated by faith are the parables of the talents and of the pounds addressed.

3. *Then What?*

Believers are not left in the dark as to how the Lord wants interest upon His investment of talents and gifts. The Word of God sheds light upon the ways in which interest accrues. God Himself connects our liberation with obedience to His commandments: "I am the Lord your God, who brought you out of the land of Egypt, out of the house of bondage. You shall have no other gods before me..." (Ex. 20:2-3). Liberation is under the Law, not from the Law: "Think not," the Christ says, "that I have come to abolish the law and the prophets; I have come not to abolish them but to fulfill them. For truly, I say to you, till heaven and earth pass away, not an iota, not a dot, will pass from the law until all is accomplished" (Matt. 5:17).

The commandments are summarized in the divine requirements to love God above all and our neighbors as ourselves (Luke 10:27). These are the twin guides to producing interest upon God's investment in ourselves.

The motif of investment-return appears in the Great Commission of the New Testament. The Apostles are mandated by the Christ to build His Church. First, they are to preach the good news (gospel) of liberation. Those who believe the good news are joined to the Church through baptism. And the Church is then obliged to teach them all that the Lord commands, which is how to produce a return upon God's investment in them (Matt. 28:19-20). And what the Lord commands is nothing else than what was summarized by the commandments given Israel after liberation from Egypt, and expounded by the Prophets throughout Israel's history—and further applied by the Apostolic epistles to the New Testament Church.

4. *God's Agents*

Like any prudent investor, God does not leave His return to chance. He pursues it. And His agent in this pursuit is His Church, where good stewardship is taught and practiced.

B. CONSCIENCE

Stewardship has a watchful monitor in the conscience.

Consider carefully, therefore, what the conscience does.

We do not say, "what the conscience *is*." Fruitless hours of speculation can be spent on what conscience *is*. It can be questioned whether or not all persons have a conscience, and if so whether it is acquired by birth or developed by environment. Avoid such detours by focusing upon how conscience behaves, what it does, and why that can be enlisted in diaconal service.

1. *What Conscience Does*

The term "conscience" implies "knowing together," or "knowing with," at one and the same time: from "con" meaning *with* and "science" meaning knowledge.

What, then, is known together by conscience? Two things: 1) the divine Law, spelled out in the Ten Commandments and inscribed by God upon the human heart as part of the divine Image in each human being; and, 2) the action one has done, or contemplates doing; the thoughts and purposes one entertains; in short, all behavior. Conscience brings Law and conduct together, and judges behavior by the Law. Conscience is the inner courtroom where God's Word and our conduct meet for judgment. Conscience is God's witness in each human heart: "...what the law requires is written on their hearts, while their conscience also bears witness..." (Rom. 2:15). Paul is here speaking of those to whom the Law did not come by special revelation, the Gentiles.

Conscience monitors behavior, makes demands upon it in the name of the Law. And in response, the believer can strive to keep his conscience clear of accusation against him by seeking to obey God's Law—and here conscience becomes ally to the believer, to the Church and to her diaconate. St. Paul says to the Roman governor Felix: "So I always take pains to have a clear conscience toward God and toward men" (Act. 24:16). That is to say, the Christian always takes pains to love, which is obedience to the Law.

2. *Bridge to the Particular*

Conscience plays a unique role in the obedient life.

It is often said that the Bible falls short of particulars in laying down regulations for Christian obedience. We are never expressly told, for example, how much we may keep for ourselves of all the goods which God gives us. We are not informed as to whether money should be given to one charity or to another, or whether it is right to enjoy good food and drink while many starve. The Bible declines to be an ethical recipe book. The Word only reveals general mandates and universal commandments.

Why?

Because God provides conscience to be the bridge from the general and universal Law to the particular act. Conscience is, so to speak, the elbow where the vertical command coming down from God governs the horizontal deed done among men.

The Bible is geared to conscience. The Word is addressed to conscience, and should be preached to conscience. Out of the struggle to do the revealed will of God in daily living, conscience emerges ever more sensitive and helpful. Conscience is the agent of Christian maturity.

3. *Always Reliable?*

It is easy to dispute the trustworthiness of conscience. "Let your conscience be your guide" is indeed not always a guarantee that what follows is in full accord with divine Law. The conscience requires a constant tutor—the Word of God. Believers bring conscience to the worship service to school it the better in awakening response to the Law—the version written on the conscience vibrating in harmony with the preaching of what is written in the Scriptures.

Estranged from the Church, and indifferent to the Bible, conscience may indeed become more and more wayward and less and less reliable: "And since they did not see fit to acknowledge God, God gave them up to a base mind and to improper conduct" (Rom. 1:28).

But aroused again and again by the Word preached, tutored by the Word studied, and disciplined by an alert eldership, the believer's conscience serves as the living voice of the Word, "accusing or else excusing" what he thinks, says, and does (Rom. 2:15, KJV).

Conscience is there. We need not, and could not, create it. But how exciting a challenge to enlist its voice in our efforts to serve the Christ through obedience to the divine Law in the form of good stewardship.

Chapter 11.

THE MYSTERY OF POVERTY

"The Lord makes poor and makes rich" (I Sam. 2:7).

Could not God immediately feed all the world's hungry?

Indeed, He could!

This is evident from the miracles done by Jesus with the loaves and fishes. He reminds His disciples: "Do you not remember the five loaves of the five thousand (Matt. 14:17-21), and how many baskets you gathered? Or the seven loaves of the four thousand (Matt. 15:34-38), and how many baskets you gathered?" (Matt. 16:9-10). Twice the Lord multiplied a lad's lunch into a meal fed to thousands of men and women, with plenty left over.

God fed Israel with manna, rained from the sky in the wilderness, and even varied the diet with the meat of quail (Ex. 16). He instructed ravens to feed the prophet Elijah with bread and meat, morning and evening; and provided that the supply of meal and oil should not fail in the home of the widow of Zarephath "for many days" (I Kings 17:6, 8-16).

There is more than enough evidence in Scripture to assure us that God could, at will, satisfy human need around the globe.

But He does not.

Why not?

Because the needy serve God's purpose, and have their own recompense for so doing.

1. *God's Purpose*

How shall those who truly love the Lord manifest their love for Him in deeds? How shall believers give their Savior material expression of their love when, in fact, all is already His and He, being perfect, needs nothing?

God provides the needy to solve this problem. He wills to be sought, found, and served in the poor. This is clear from what has already been said about investment in heaven. It is clear, too, from the parable of the Last Judgment, where the Lord equates gifts made to the poor as made to Him: "Truly, I say to you, as you did it to one of the least of these my brethren, you did it to me" (Matt. 25:40).

The poor and needy are God's surrogates. We serve Him through them. That is why there are poor in God's world. And to compensate for the burden of poverty, as we shall see, God gives the needy special blessing.

2. *Secular Explanations*

The secular mind attempts many explanations for poverty. Behind them all, the Bible gives us but one fundamental account: "The Lord makes poor..." (I Sam. 2:7).

The difference between the secular explanations and the Bible's account is of crucial importance to believers, in discerning that the poor are not so much a problem as an answer. God provides the needy so that the Christian can answer the question: why give? and why give in money and material goods?

Secular explanations account for poverty from some inferred cause, like: the poor are lazy, the poor are shiftless, the poor cannot handle money, do not know how to save, cannot restrain their desires, lack employable skills, can't hold a job, won't take orders, are victimized by their own sub-culture, etc. All of which may be, indeed, God's means to poverty. And, as secondary causes, they do provide Christians with the challenge to set right what can be amended. There will always be poor enough in the world so that the Lord can bless every serious effort to prevent poverty. But the underlying meaning of poverty is the Lord's will to provide opportunity to the true believer to display love in deed. This becomes evident in the fact that countless millions of poor humans slave at jobs from dawn to dusk and remain poverty-stricken just the same. God makes poor...

Jesus tells a parable (Matt. 20:1-16) which enforces what is revealed through

Samuel. A householder, Jesus says, goes out in the marketplace to hire laborers for his vineyard. Some he finds and hires early in the morning, some later in the day, and still others well toward evening. At day's end, the householder instructs his steward to pay each worker the very same wage. Some who had labored through the heat of day complain that those who had worked but a little get the same reward. To which the householder (God) responds: "Am I not allowed to do what I choose with what belongs to me?" (Matt. 20:15).

God, the Creator and owner of all things, does His will with the world's goods. He makes poor and rich, by giving and withholding what is His own.

We note, in passing, that poverty is the stuff of which revolution is made. Marxism rests its appeal on the misery of the proletariat. The Bible, too, has a response to that misery: obedience among the rich and powerful to the commandments of God.

Moses takes account of this option in addressing the Church as it appeared in the form of Israel: "But there will be no poor among you...if only you will obey the voice of the Lord your God, being careful to do all this commandment which I command you this day" (Deut. 15:4-5). This, then, becomes the New Testament Church's ideal: there need be no poverty around the world, if only God's commandment to love were universally obeyed. Such should be the goal of missions and evangelism!

God does, indeed, make poor. So the Scriptures teach. But He does so, as it were, against His will. God's command to love Him above all is fulfilled in that love for neighbor which makes the elimination of poverty its prime goal.

Jesus is, alas, so certain that the commandment of God will not be universally obeyed, that He can say: "The poor you always have with you" (John 12:8). Marxism will not, either, scourge poverty from the face of the globe. As Moses himself had acknowledged: "For the poor will never cease out of the land..." (Deut. 15:11)—that is, on account of our disobedience.

3. *Divine Compensation*

God goes out of His way, however, throughout the Bible, to reveal an intense concern for the poor whom He provides as opportunity to the rich, in ways like these:

a. God hears their cries of distress: "For the Lord hears the needy..." (Ps. 69:33). "Hears" means, in Scripture, "acts upon". God responds to the pleas of the oppressed and needy. Many a head lies restless upon its pillow because God has heard the groans of those oppressed by its owner. Many a business failure took first root in deceit against the unwary. God hears when the victims of injustice cry to Him.

b. God supplies spiritual strength to the poor so that they may transcend their lives of grinding hardship: "For thou hast been a stronghold to the poor, a strength to the needy in his distress" (Is. 25:4). The endurance of the oppressed in the face of apparently insurmountable odds is God-given. The peace that may pervade a poor dwelling descends from above. The sweet sleep of the dead-tired may contrast with the restlessness of the rich. God makes poor, and compensates in His own way for their tragedy.

c. Though poverty commonly affords little hope of temporal escape for those caught in its toils, God promises that "the needy shall not always be forgotten, and the hope of the poor shall not perish forever" (Ps. 9:18). The Lord lifts the eyes of the needy beyond the narrow horizons of their time-bound lives, and gives them hope which lays hold upon another, fairer world.

d. The promise given the poor is precise and explicit: "'Because the poor are despoiled, because the needy groan, I will now arise,' says the Lord; 'I will place him in the safety for which he longs'" (Ps. 12:5). The veil between time and eternity wears thin in poverty, and God lets the needy look easily beyond the narrow confines of their earthly lives. Consider the triumphant songs of the oppressed!

e. To accomplish these things among

those whom He has made poor, God endows them liberally with faith: "Has not God chosen those who are poor in the world to be rich in faith and heirs of the kingdom which He promised to those who love Him?" (Jas. 2:5). This is why the risen Christ can instruct St. John to write to the Church of Smyrna, "I know your tribulation and your poverty (but you are rich)..." (Rev. 2:9). Poor in goods, but rich in faith and sure promises!

f. It is not surprising, then, that Mary magnifies the joy of Jesus' birth by singing that the Lord has "exalted those of low degree; He has filled the hungry with good things, and the rich he has sent empty away" (Luke 1:52-53). Jesus is food of hope and promise of liberation to the poor. But those rich who will not share their goods, in Jesus' name, find nothing in the Christ for themselves. Their hands full of unshared possessions, they are sent spiritually empty away by a Lord they will not serve with their hoarded goods. And the Christ Himself confirms His mother's prediction, saying at His home in Nazareth, "the Spirit of the Lord is upon me, because he has anointed me to preach good news to the poor" (Luke 4:18)—words taken from the Prophet, said many years before (Is. 61:1). God compensates those whom He makes poor in goods with the riches of the Good News of Jesus Christ.

g. Having made the poor vulnerable to the greedy, the Lord keeps jealous watch over their treatment: "The Lord enters into judgment with the elders and princes of his people: 'It is you who have devoured the Vineyard, the spoil of the poor is in your houses. What do you mean by crushing my people, by grinding the face of the poor?'" (Is. 3:14-15). The wicked prove themselves wicked by taking advantage of those whom the Lord has made temporally defenseless: "In arrogance the wicked hotly pursue the poor...he lurks in secret like a lion in his covert; he lurks that he may seize the poor, he seizes the poor when he draws him into his net" (Ps. 10:2, 9). But God takes special note of evil done to those whom He has made poor. For that sin He destroys Sodom, raining down fire from on high (Gen. 19:24-25).

h. It was Sodom's fatal crime that she neglected the poor, and exploited those whom God had rendered weak: "Behold, this was the guilt of your sister Sodom: she and her daughters had pride, surfeit of food, and prosperous ease, but did not aid the poor and needy" (Ezek. 16:49).

4. *In Summary*

Why, then, has God made many poor, and expends such concern over them?

Believers should reflect, as they review what has been said so far, on the parable of the rich man and Lazarus (Luke 16:19-31).

What was the poor beggar doing at Dives' gate? All he asked for food was the scraps discarded from the rich man's sumptuous table. He seems to do Dives no service. He waits in vain for love expressed in charity. Then Lazarus dies, and lo, he appears in heaven!

Why?

Because, no doubt, he had richly served God's purposes by patiently bearing the heavy yoke of poverty. Lazarus accepted without complaint the burdens laid by God upon his shoulders. And what service, then, did Lazarus do for God?

He put Dives to the test.

God made Lazarus materially poor so that Dives might be spiritually blessed. Opportunity to show love for God in doing good to Lazarus was on Dives' very doorstep. He could not come or go from his residence without observing the knock of God upon his hard heart.

Dives failed the test. He, too, like Lazarus, died—and went straight to hell!

The Lord could not more graphically portray the role of the poor in God's world. At issue in this drama, which is played everywhere around the world, was not so much Lazarus' need as Dives' soul. At issue everywhere that poverty appears is God's test of man's soul. For the poor it is a question of patient endurance of God's yoke. For the rich it is a question of love working through material goods.

And the judgment is sure: "Depart from me, ye cursed, into everlasting fire prepared for the devil and his angels. For I was hungry and ye gave me no food, I was thirsty, and ye gave me no drink..." (Matt. 25:42).

The mystery of poverty is that God uses the needy to stand in His stead among all the nations of the world. Because their yoke is burdensome, God lightens their plight with excess of faith, hope, and love. And through them God tests:

1. Those whose service to Him is in talk only, mere lip-service.

2. Those who cannot resist the temptation to take advantage of the weak.

3. Those who, in their eagerness to display their love, seek Him out in the needy where He may be found, and give of their goods, time, talents, and skills to them.

Chapter 12.

THE MYSTERY OF WEALTH

"The silver is mine, and the gold is mine, says the Lord of hosts" (Hag. 2:8).

No sound perspective on the Church's duty toward the wealthy is possible apart from this revealed truth: all wealth, however acquired, is God's, let out on strictly temporary loan to whoever is its temporal possessor. So crucial is this fundamental Christian economic maxim that we repeat it, and urge that all believers be persistently reminded of the Lord's repeated declaration: "For the world and all that is in it is mine" (Ps. 50:12). Israel's King David, who himself accumulated vast public and personal sums in preparation for building the Lord's temple in Jerusalem, declares: "Both riches and honor come from thee, and thou rulest over all" (I Chron. 29:12).

Even the very effort through which anyone acquires temporal title to God's material gifts is itself His donation: "You shall remember the Lord your God, for it is he who gives you the power to get wealth'' (Deut. 8:18).

All this, we repeat, is background and context for the Church's approach to the mystery of wealth.

1. *In Exchange*

In exchange for His gifts, as we have pointed out, the Lord exacts return. God is, as we have said, a free enterpriser, demanding interest on His loans to mankind in proportion to the gift: "Everyone to whom much is given, of him will much be required" (Luke 12:48).

But how shall the recipient of wealth know what is "required" of him in exchange for its temporal use?

Only those who ask this question seriously receive an answer: "It is written in the prophet, 'And they shall all be taught of God' " (John 6:45; Jesus is quoting Isaiah 54:13).

And how does God now teach?

By His Word, the Holy Scripture, most authoritatively as that Word is preached *in* the Church by those ordained *by* the Church to the task: "And how are they to hear without a preacher? And how can men preach unless they are sent?" (Rom. 10:14-15).

To use a Biblical illustration, the world is the Lord's vineyard, and "Who plants a vineyard without eating any of its fruit?" (I Cor. 9:7). In a more restricted sense, we may transpose the language of the prophet to say, using "Church" instead of "Israel": "And the vineyard of the Lord of Hosts is the Church, and

the members of it are his pleasant planting"
(Is. 5:7).

It is within the Church that the question
is most seriously asked: how shall we know
what the divine Owner of the vineyard whose
fruits we enjoy "requires" of us? It is within
the Church that the answer is seriously
supplied: "Thy word is a lamp to my feet and
a light to my path" (Ps. 119:105). It is within
the Church that the call goes out: "O house of
Jacob, come, let us walk in the light of the
Lord" (Is. 2:5). And it is within the Church
that the scientific light shed by economics
upon the uses of wealth is set in the light of the
inspired Word: "...in thy light shall we see (our)
light" (Ps. 36:9).

2. *What does The Church Say?*

The Church says—or should say—concerning what God requires of those whom He
has made wealthy only—and all—what the
Bible says. Human research and investigation,
however thorough, will not suffice. Classical or
Marxist economics is not enough, and leads
astray if not set in His light. The tenant cannot
dictate to the Landlord the conditions of his
labor or nature of his rent. The tenant—man—
can only strive to learn God's rules and to do
them lest he face eternal eviction. For if the
Landlord's will is ignored, His reaction to such
rebellion is sure: "What will the owner of the
vineyard do? He will come and destroy the
tenants and give the vineyard to others"

(Mark 12:9). And, indeed, the inexorable passage of time brings new tenants into the vineyard and old tenants to inevitable judgment, where ignorance will be no excuse for disobedience.

What, then, does the Church have to say about wealth and its responsibilities?

This question can be answered only on two levels: 1) the teaching of the Scriptures on economic and other matters can be and has been organized into general perspectives, but 2) there is no "Christian economics" which can coerce what the pulpit will speak to the rich—or to the poor. The pulpit is free. Its freedom is guaranteed by obedience to the Word, and to the Word alone. No economics can antecedently prescribe what the Word will say to the rich—or to anyone else—as a text is exegetically applied to the life of the congregation. The sermon is—or ought to be—an adventure. The Word always runs far ahead of where the Church is, and the obedient pulpit brings tidings from tomorrow to today. No "Christian" economics dictates content to preaching; it is formulated in the preaching.

We will, therefore, suggest Biblical perspectives on the obligations of wealth to its Donor, but a living Word can only be spoken into the ear of the rich from the lips of a faithful pastor. Indeed, the Word preached at large to the congregation is particularized in the ear of each who *hears* its syllables. What is said by the pulpit, from the Word, to the wealthy is heard by each in exact proportion to his capacity to hear: "He who has ears to hear, let him hear" (Matt. 11:15). So the Lord expressed the thought we are wishing here to stress, namely that the Word spoken comes alive only in those able truly to "hear" what the Lord is saying on the lips of His ordained servant.

And who, then, comes with ears able to hear?

Only whoever comes desiring, passionately desiring, to have the Word of the Lord addressed to himself: "...seek the Lord your God, and you will find him, if you search after him with all your heart and with all your soul" (Deut. 4:29).

The Word truly preached will be heard by all truly desirous to know the will of the Landlord. He will hear who knows himself a tenant for limited duration, eager to know, because eager to do, the Landlord's good pleasure before He returns to demand an accounting of the use made of His good gifts (Matt. 21:33, 40). Such tenants seek out where the Word is faithfully preached, and will hear what the Lord requires of their stewardship.

But he who is rebellious at heart, determined to dispose of "his" wealth as he alone sees fit, will not really hear the Lord's Word even if he forever attend upon its proclamation: "The word of the Lord came to me, 'Son of man, you dwell in the midst of a rebellious house, who have eyes to see, but see not, who have ears to hear, but hear not, for they are a rebellious house' '' (Ezek. 12:1-3). Rebels in the vineyard will demand, or devise, their own science of economics, claiming that the Word is economically silent or illiterate. And to them it is!

3. *Why To Each?*

Does the preached Word in fact speak to all while being heard (if heard at all) by each?

Indeed, how else can it be? For each of God's image-bearers is unique. If no two snowflakes are ever alike, will two persons ever be? Each of us is a first and only edition. So God acknowledges, and addresses us individually in the Word said to all but particularized by each.

Do you feel that in our mechanized society all slots are alike, and rob everyone of individuality? Anyone can push the broom, bake the pie, tend the machine, occupy the office, farm the land, or teach the class? Maybe so. But that is not the issue when our God-ordained uniqueness is in view. Anyone, or almost anyone, can do your job, but only you can accumulate what doing the job does to the doer! The work may be the same, but each "you" who does the work is unique. And the self that emerges from a lifetime of experience is unlike any other self made by God. It's not what we *do* that passes into eternity, but who we become by doing. And who we finally are is the living deposit of each day's doing, either in the light of the Word of God or the twilight of the word of man. God meets us uniquely because otherwise He would not meet us at all. He seeks out each of us—by name: "He who has an ear, let him hear what the Spirit says to the churches. To him who conquers I will give some of the hidden manna, and I will give him a white stone, with a new name written on the stone which no one knows except him who receives it" (Rev. 2:17). Despite appearances to the contrary, life is opportunity to individuality, and the Word which is addressed to all celebrates the uniqueness of each by speaking to each where he lives.

The Bible does not permit, therefore, simplistic solutions to the mystery of riches, like these:

1. That the rich should give all their wealth away. The Bible nowhere prescribes this.

2. That the Bible depreciates wealth. On the contrary, the Bible equates wealth with divine blessing.

3. That the Bible views having great possessions as evidence of lack of charity. God rather embraces those to whom He has given wealth from the age of the Patriarchs to the present.

The Word speaks uniquely to each of us to ward off such simplistic exegeses.

4. *Abuse of Texts*

We take note of certain Biblical texts

often mistakenly employed to resolve the mystery of wealth, like these:

a. We have already observed that a rich young man, often called the rich young ruler, approaches Jesus with a question: "Teacher, what good deed must I do, to have eternal life?" The Lord points him to the Law. The young man claims to have kept the Law from his youth. Then Jesus adds: "If you would be perfect, go, sell what you possess and give it to the poor, and you will have treasure in heaven; and come, follow me" (Matt. 19:16, 21).

Can only the poor follow him? And is this a mandate laid on all who are rich: "Go, sell what you possess and give it to the poor"?

It would be recklessly simplistic so to interpret the story.

Such total divestiture was not required of Zacchaeus, chief tax collector of Jericho. Zacchaeus was blessed by the same Lord who admonished the rich young man to sell all, when Zacchaeus declared: "Behold, the half of my goods I give to the poor..." (Luke 19:8).

Sell all, then? Or half? Or...?

We are saying that no generalizations can be derived from simplistic exegesis of selected texts. Clearly, the Lord dealt then as His Word does today, uniquely with each who come seeking direction for the use of his wealth.

Joseph of Arimathea was "a rich man" (Matt. 27:57), who fulfilled prophecy (Is. 53:9) because his riches gave him access to Pilate to secure the body of Jesus for burial in Joseph's new-hewn tomb. Jesus Himself and His disciples were supported by those "who provided for them out of their means" (Luke 8:3), and Paul is befriended by the wealthy on his journeys (Acts 16:40, for example). Abraham and all the Patriarchs were very rich and companions of God, as was King David who was both rich and the prototype of Jesus.

In short, no simplistic inference can be carried over from the advice given the rich young man to the obligations of all the rich who seek to please God. Rather, it becomes obvious that the Word of the Lord addresses, all across history, each of the wealthy in a unique way.

b. Immediately after the rich young man rejects Jesus' advice, the Lord has the following discussion with His disciples: "And Jesus said to his disciples, 'Truly, I say to you, it will be hard for a rich man to enter the kingdom of heaven. Again I tell you, it is easier for a camel to go through the eye of a needle than for a rich man to enter the kingdom of God.' When the disciples heard this, they were greatly astonished, saying, 'Who then can be saved?' But Jesus looked at them and said to them, 'With men this is impossible, but with God all things are possible' " (Matt. 19:23-26).

It is easy to infer from this conversation that only those who shrug off all their riches can squeeze through the strait gate onto the narrow road that leads to eternal life (Matt. 7:14). An easy, but simplistically mistaken inference.

Why were the disciples "astonished"? Had they hitherto supposed that the rich were guaranteed first entrance upon the Kingdom? And, therefore, with their exclusion no one at all would make it? So they seem to say: "Who then (if not the rich) can be saved?" And perhaps this was their mistaken assumption: first the rich, blessed by God with abundance, and then the poor, less favored from above. But "Jesus looked at them," St. Matthew tells us. Why? Is it a look of surprise? Of disappointment? How little they understand of His coming, and teaching! Can riches ever pry open the gates to the Kingdom by being given away? Does wealth unlock the strait gate? Of course not!

Entrance upon the Kingdom is quite irrespective of wealth. It is by faith revealed in obedience, also a gift of God: "With men this is impossible, but with God all things are possible"—that is, only God can make the dead soul live, and change the alien into a true citizen of the Kingdom and a good steward of His blessings.

That the temptations of wealth do indeed threaten entrance upon the Kingdom is true. We shall take note of that below. But neither the abundance nor the absence of riches, as such, governs eternal destiny. The soul passes through the eye of the needle by grace, not by selling all it has.

c. "Do not lay up for yourselves treasures on earth..." (Matt. 6:19).

Is this an admonition against the acquisition of wealth?

It is, if the acquisition is "for yourselves"!

It is, then, if the purpose is for saying, "Soul, you have ample goods laid up for many years; take your ease, eat, drink, be merry" (Luke 12:19). Such acquisition characterizes the "fool" (Luke 12:20).

But wealth legitimately acquired may also become capital which, in a free society, has the power to organize human energies into productive enterprise. Goods and services useful to God's world are called into existence by energies assembled and structured for productive efficiency by capital and those characterized by integrity and qualified by talent to accumulate and manage it. Such accumulation of treasure need not be, though it can be, solely "for yourselves". It is not forbidden by Scripture.

Still more, as already pointed out, wealth is power. Would that much more of such power were put to the service of the Kingdom by those who have it, and who hear the Word of God addressed to them! The hope of the weak for justice is largely dependent upon the power of wealth, and upon its influence enlisted for them by the rich who hear the Word of the Lord. The support of Kingdom causes depends heavily upon the wealthy. Social change in directions pointed by divine Law is most readily, and bloodlessly, accomplished through the power of sanctified wealth.

d. "Son, remember that you in your lifetime received your good things, and Lazarus in like manner evil things; but now he is comforted here, and you are in anguish" (Luke 16:25).

The speaker is Abraham, who is in heaven comforting Lazarus the poor beggar who lay unattended at rich Dives' gate and now enjoys the bliss of eternity. He is addressing Dives who once "was clothed in purple and fine linen and who feasted sumptuously every day" (Luke 16:19), and now, after death, is in hell.

Does this mean an antithesis: rich here, poor there; poor here, rich there?

Hardly, for the very Abraham who speaks had been himself very rich, had enjoyed his "good things" on earth, and now appears in heaven.

Time is indeed the vestibule to eternity. Dives gets where he is by reason of his behavior—or rather, misbehavior—in time. But was hell, then, the "compensation" for his riches?

No, for God Himself is the donor of riches. Hell is Dives' destiny because he accounted God's gifts as solely for his own sensual benefit. He arrives in hell not for what he had but for what he lacked: "But if any one of you has the world's goods and sees his brother in need, yet closes his heart against him, how does God's love abide in him?" (I John 3:17). Blind of eye, lacking love, Dives does not see Lazarus' need. Deaf of ear, lacking love, Dives does not hear Lazarus' weakening pleas. Hard of heart, lacking in love, Dives eats and drinks and makes merry like the fool who says in his heart, "There is no God" (Ps. 14:1)—and spends eternity, therefore, in keeping with his profession.

But it is lack of love, and not God's good gifts to him in his lifetime, that determines Dives' destiny. The Bible does not teach that wealth, in itself, is cursed by compensation with evil after death.

5. *The Mystery*

But this is the mystery of wealth: that God's good gift can so readily become man's idol. And in the service of the gift instead of the Giver man goes the broad way to destruction (Matt. 7:13).

Wealth may come in many ways. Seemingly, it may be, by accident or luck, one comes into a fortune. Or by inheritance. Or through hard work, or shrewd investment, or careful saving. Who would know, without the light of the Word, that behind the scenes the ultimate Giver of all riches is God!

Wealth may come in many forms. We concentrate in this chapter on material goods. But there are gifts of talent, of beauty, of warmth of heart, of skills, of qualities of spirit—many that money cannot buy, and some far more rare than money, like artistic abilities. But always the gift can become the god, God's good perverted by man unto his damnation, "because they exchanged the truth about God for a lie and worshiped and served the creature rather than the Creator, who is blessed forever! Amen" (Rom. 1:25).

The Word, therefore, surrounds wealth with warnings, to which we shall attend. But we stress the point here that these warnings do not include the requirement that he who is blessed with abundance is thereby required to give it all away. There are, we repeat, no such simplistic alternatives for avoiding the burden of responsible use of God's good gifts. The key to responsible employment of wealth comes from the same Hand that provides the goods—it is in His inspired Word, given to the Church for proclamation to congregation and world. There the mystery of wealth is set in the context of obedience to the Giver.

6. *Mistaken Options*

Not only are some Biblical texts misinterpreted as regards the use of riches, as suggested above, but we believe that what are today called "theologies of liberation" also abuse Scripture for mistaken purposes. We take brief note of this error.

Theology of liberation has followed upon theology of revolution, both largely expounded in Central and South America, though with European roots, and both generally developed by Roman Catholic theologians. The motivation is sincere, and the point of departure very real:

a. Theology of liberation grows out of the observation and experience of human misery and of man's grim inhumanity to man. The awesome misery of the utterly destitute—the mystery of poverty—so common in the Third World provokes pity, rage, and despair. Pity for the helpless, miserable destitute, unable to provide for themselves and, still worse, for their starving and stunted children. Rage against those wealthy enough to help, but coldly, brutally unwilling to do so, and against those utterly indifferent to it all. And despair that so often the Church seems so little concerned, so cowardly, and so ineffective. Quite naturally, those who cannot sleep with the moans of misery echoing in their hearts seek license in the Scriptures for revolution sometimes, seek cooperation with Marxists to achieve it. Using the models of Israel's liberation from Egypt—the Exodus—and of Christ's triumph over the power of darkness at Calvary and through the empty tomb—Christ the Liberator—the theology of liberation seeks to take history into its own revolutionary hands.

Starting from the Bible, these theologians sooner or later subdue the Word to their own ultimate designs. Theology of liberation is not obedient response to the abuse of wealth.

b. Consider, for example, this: if we can be appalled, as we should be, by human degradation, how much more must heaven be outraged by man's perversion of God's gifts into instruments of exploitation, how much more must God be anguished by human selfishness and unconcern. We may be sure, therefore, that the Bible has always reckoned seriously with precisely the gross iniquities that drive sensitive souls into plotting revolution. Indeed, the Bible always has: "Vengeance is mine, and recompense..." (Deut. 32:35). "For we know him who said, 'Vengeance is mine, I will repay.' And again, 'The Lord will judge his people.' It is a fearful thing to fall into the hands of the living God" (Heb. 10:30-31). Time and again, the Word of the Lord assures us that "The Lord is not slow about his promise as some count slowness..." (I Pet. 3:9). The day of judgment, far more terrible than any mundane revolution, awaits the merciless: "Then he will say to those at his left hand, 'Depart from me, you cursed, into the eternal fire prepared for the devil and his angels; for I was hungry and you gave me no food, I was thirsty and you gave me no drink, I was a stranger and you did not welcome me, naked and you did not clothe me, sick and in prison and you did not visit me.' Then they also will answer, 'Lord, when did we see thee hungry or thirsty or a stranger or naked or sick or in prison and did not minister to thee?' Then he will answer them, 'Truly, I say to you, as you did it not to one of the least of these, you did it not to me.' And they will go away into eternal punishment..." (Matt. 25:41-46). The Lord is aware, far more keenly aware than are we, of man's inhumanity to man. His judgment already begins in the unease which the inhumane endure, in the absence of joy which beclouds their seemingly happiest moments, and His judgment concludes in eternal damnation.

What is of crucial importance to the theologian is not revolution but proclamation. Are the rich courageously warned, again and again, that something worse than revolt threatens them if they hoard God's goods against human need, and use God's gifts to exploit God's children: "I tell you, my friends, do not fear those who kill the body, and later that have no more that they can do. But I will warn you whom to fear: fear him who, after he has killed, has power to cast into hell; yes, I tell you, fear him!" (Luke 12:4-5). This is, fear God! Let the Church so warn mankind against the "day of wrath when God's righteous judgment will be revealed. For he will render to every man according to his works: to those who by patience in well-doing seek for glory and honor and immortality, he will give eternal life; but for those who are factious and do not obey the truth, but obey wickedness, there will be wrath and fury" (Rom. 2:5-8). Let theologians demand such preaching!

c. *Political* revolution, which seeks freedom for proclamation and for obedience according to conscience, *is justified* by Scripture, and has given the Western world the liberties we now enjoy. But *economic* revolution, along Marxist lines, has enthroned tyranny wherever it has been successful, and has destroyed the freedom of preaching without which a society becomes it own prison. Marxist revolution has sometimes provided bread at the expense of liberty, but the world observes that the Solzhenitsyns who speak for multitudes declare "that man does not live by bread alone, but by everything that proceeds out of the mouth of the Lord" (Deut. 8:3), quoted by Christ against the Devil, (Matt. 4:4). Theology of liberation, so long as it substitutes economic for political Exodus, only points to the substitution of one tyranny for another.

d. Finally, theology of liberation via Marxist revolt assumes that evil has an explanation and, therefore, a rational cure. This is not a Biblical, but rather a secular premise. Evil surfaces in human exploitation and callous greed. Evil tramples on the destitute in the persons of the greedy. But evil is without explanation. Evil has parentage—the Evil One —but no ground. Evil responds to no "why" or "wherefore". Hard heart, blind eye, deaf ear—the origin of these is hidden in "the mystery of iniquity" (II Thess. 2:7). The Bible assigns no cause for human depravity which may be isolated by social or psychological or economic relations, and then assumes that abolition of such relations cures evil at its source. The dimensions of this mistake are evident in the new crop of evil which Communist tyranny so abundantly produces.

The Bible knows but one source of man's inhumanity to man. It is the depraved human heart. And the Bible knows but one cure for depraved hearts—the indwelling of Christ, via His Word, which makes new what was depraved: "Therefore, if anyone is in Christ, he is a new creation; the old has passed away, behold, the new has come" (II Cor. 5:17).

We are not endorsing the substitution of "faith" for obedience, nor the preaching of heaven as substitute for social justice. We are saying that the Bible sets the Word of God, faithfully and fully and courageously preached, in the fore of man's pursuit of social righteousness. The world may give up on the Word of God and turn to the words of Marx. But the Church can never forget that the only lastingly liberating power available to man in history is the Bible truly preached: "For as the rain and the snow come down from heaven, and return not thither but water the earth, making it bring forth and sprout, giving seed to the sower and bread to the eater, so shall my word be that goes forth from my mouth; it shall not return to me empty, but it shall accomplish that which I purpose, and prosper in the thing for which I sent it" (Is. 55:10-11). This is the Word of the Lord. Simon Peter confesses to Jesus: "Lord, to whom (else) shall we go? You have the words of eternal life..." (John 6:68). But to those who despair of the Word's power to effect social change, there is the Lord's warning: "He who rejects me and does not receive my sayings has a judge: the word that I have spoken will be his judge on the last day" (John 12:48).

Either the Church and her theologians trust the power of the Word to transform social evil, or that Word will on the last day judge the Church herself for apostasy.

We therefore believe that the Word fearlessly preached, from every pulpit free to speak it, is far more productive of social righteousness than the threat or even the success of Marxist revolt.

Moreover, we believe that the Exodus is not the symbol of successful *economic* rebellion. It was the passage from bondage to the opportunity freely to serve Jehovah. The Exodus is a model for political, but not for economic, revolution. The goal of the Exodus is the right to worship: "And you shall say to Pharaoh," God says to Moses, "Thus says the Lord, Israel is my first-born son, and I say to

you, 'Let my son go that he may serve me'"
(Ex. 4:22-23). And the Exodus in time produces
the proclamation: "...proclaim liberty throughout the land and to all the inhabitants thereof"
(Lev. 25:10). To such revolution, the kind that
gave democracy to one country after another in
the West after the Reformation, the Bible
lends support. And for such revolution the
Exodus serves as a model, as does the Christ
who liberates us also from Egyptian bondage,
that we may freely serve Him.

For the path out of Egypt leads directly
to Sinai where God reveals why He liberates
His people, then and now: "I am the Lord your
God, who brought you out of the land of
Egypt, out of the house of bondage. You shall
have no other gods before me..." (Ex. 20:2-3).

We observe, then, that theology of liberation is not the Bible's approach to resolving
the obligation of riches to the God who gives
them. At the same time, we believe that
the Bible does endorse political revolution
where it is necessary to secure freedom of the
pulpit and liberty of obedience according to
conscience.

What, then, is the Bible's approach to
man and his wealth?

7. *Biblical Perspectives - General*

What the Lord requires of each of His
children as return upon His gifts to them will
be specifically heard, we have observed, by
each in the Spirit-guided conjunction of Word

proclaimed, of willing ear, and in the light of circumstances peculiar to each listener.

But the Bible does provide certain perspectives which everyone can employ for teaching himself and helping other believers see the obligations of wealth. First, general perspectives like these:

a. The Christian must seek to put himself and all his time, talents, and goods at God's disposal. Not at God's disposal as we wish or think that to be, but at God's disposal as He graciously reveals His will in His Word. This is the true believer's response to the First of the Great Commandments: "You shall love the Lord your God with all your heart, and with all your soul, and with all your strength, and with all your mind..." (Luke 10:27; Deut. 6:5). To love God is to obey Him. The believer obeys; the obedient believe. Of this, rich Abraham is prime example. Thus to love God according to the First Commandment is deliberately to put oneself and all one has under His directives as revealed in His Word. The wealthy who turn to the Church—its preaching ministry, its ruling eldership, its serving diaconate—for guidance from the Scriptures as to appropriate use of their goods, set themselves in the right posture for doing good stewardship.

A parallel, in the Church, of such docility —teachableness—appears in the relation between the preaching and the Word. The obedient pulpit serves the inspired text even as the preacher employs his own words to expound and apply it. "He who hears you," the Lord says of such preaching, "hears me" (Luke 10:16). How do human words become God's? By *obedience* to the text. The preacher whose sole desire is to obey the Word of the Lord as he shapes his thoughts, and phrases his sentences, attains this awesome authority: what he says in obedience to the text, God in Christ says! Similarly, in close parallel, the believer who submits what he does with his wealth to governance by the Word may know that what he does God is doing with, and through, him. This is obedience to the First Great Commandment.

b. A second general Biblical perspective is opened by the Second of the Great Commandments: "thou shalt love thy neighbor as thyself" (Luke 10:27; Lev. 19:18). Obedience to God results in service to neighbor. Love of God is authenticated by love for man. It is striking that St. Paul sets this priority in his great hymn to love in the first letter to Corinth: first love, that is to say, the will to obey the Word, and then all else; but, lacking love, all else too becomes nothing: "If I give away all I have, and if I deliver my body to be burned, but have not love, I gain nothing" (I Cor. 13:3).

The Word of God works, as it were, by indirection. It achieves one end by seeming to aim at another. Seeking the open hand and generous heart, the Word points us to love.

Given love, all else follows; lacking love, no good can come. Therefore, the Apostle concludes: "Make love your aim..." (I Cor. 14:1). Therefore all that is commanded us in the Law is summed up in: Love...! The Church which preaches love, as duty to obey rather than as warmth of emotion, is a Church where the fruits of love will be achieved as by-product.

The Two Great Commandments, therefore, are the general Biblical guidelines for the proper use of all God's gifts.

8. *Biblical Perspectives - Specific*

In the context of the Commandments, the Bible lays down more specific perspectives on the proper use of wealth:

a. There are repeated warnings against letting possessions become masters rather than remaining servants:

1) "No one can serve two masters; for either he will hate the one and love the other, or he will be devoted to the one and despise the other. You cannot serve God and mammon" (Matt. 6:24).

Man is capable of two loves, two servitudes, but not at the same time. He can love, that is obey, God in the service of neighbor, or he can love gold in the service of self. The Word of the Lord comes to oblige us to choose, not only once but day after day: "Behold, I set before you this day a blessing and a curse: the blessing, if you obey the commandments of the Lord your God, which I command you this day, and the curse, if you do not obey the commandments of the Lord your God, but turn aside from the way which I command you this day, to go after other gods which you have not known" (Deut. 11:26-28).

The same hand may grasp with greed *and* give a smattering away, but the heart can only serve one master: God or self. Moses puts the alternatives again: "I call heaven and earth to witness against you this day, that I have set before you life and death, blessing and curse; therefore choose life, that you and your descendants may live, loving the Lord your God, obeying his voice, and cleaving to him; for that means life to you and length of days..." (Deut. 30:19-20). Think not that this choice was only presented, ages ago, to people long since gone from the face of the earth. It is precisely the choice set before us now, and always: "therefore choose life"! Surrender yourself and all you have to the will of the Lord as revealed in His Word! For not to serve Him *is* to serve the Adversary. The heart can have but one guiding star. There is no dual citizenship as between the Kingdom of Heaven and...another.

2) Riches not put to God's disposal threaten the very roots of the spiritual life. In His parable of the sower, Christ teaches that the Word once received may be choked out by "the cares of this world and the deceitfulness in riches" (Matt. 13:22). Wealth does not itself stand as neutral over against the soul. What is not freely committed to control by the Word quickly becomes enemy to the Word, and threatens to throttle the voice of the Lord and darken the light of His revelation. Enemies of obedience are the fingers of greed and the showy tinsel of affluence.

3) St. Paul goes so far as to charge that "the love of money is the root of all evils" (I Tim. 6:10). Here, as elsewhere, the Scripture is not condemning wealth as such. It is the *love* of money that is condemned. For love always makes of its object an end in itself.

4) The Wisdom of Proverbs reinforces the same truth: "Do not toil to acquire wealth; be wise enough to desist" (Prov. 23:4). Once again, warned against here is the pursuit of wealth as an end in itself, or as solely the means of gratifying one's own selfish desires.

5) Summary: Biblical passages like these, which might be multiplied, establish perspectives upon wealth in terms of two absolute alternatives: either, 1) we place our goods of all kinds at God's disposal under His Word, or 2) these good gifts become an intolerable burden weighting the soul toward hell and hardening the heart against all appeals from the needy.

b. The Bible also opens suggestive perspectives upon specific economic relations; we instance but an illustrative few:

1) *Pay wages promptly and in full:* "Behold, the wages of the laborers who mowed

your fields, which you kept back by fraud, cry out; and the cries of the harvesters have reached the ears of the Lord of hosts" (Jas. 5:4). This admonition of the Lord's Word is as timely today as when the Apostle penned it. All employers owe it obedience in terms of their own business affairs.

2) *Be generous:* "When you reap the harvest of your land, you shall not reap your field to its very border, neither shall you gather the gleanings after your harvest. And you shall not strip your vineyard bare, neither shall you gather the fallen grapes of your vineyard; you shall leave them for the poor and the sojourner: I am the Lord your God" (Lev. 19:9). Economic circumstances change, but God does not. Though he has every *legal* right to do so, the owner or employer is *not* to extract every penny he can—remember the needs of those employed by you, or within reach of your generosity.

3) *Be scrupulously honest:* "You shall do not wrong in judgment, in measures of length or weight or quantity. You shall have just balances, just weights, a just ephah (measure of grain), and a just hin (liquid measure): I am the Lord your God, who brought you out of the land of Egypt" (Lev. 19:35-37). The same Lord our God has brought us, too, in Christ, out of Egyptian bondage to Satan, to ourselves, and to our possessions. In Egypt anything goes, but not among those for whom

the Lord is God. Among them, there must be absolute integrity in every transaction, including refusal to buy cheap and sell dear, if no value be added in between.

4) *Pay labor what it is worth:* "I will be a swift witness...against those who oppress the hireling in his wages, the widow and the orphan..." (Hag. 2:5). Do not take advantage of the defenseless in your employ. Do not league with necessity to drive hard bargains, pay starvation wages, or demand overtime without remuneration.

5) *Avoid usury:* "You shall not lend upon interest to your brother, interest on money, interest on victuals, interest on anything that is lent for interest" (Deut. 23:19). The Church since Calvin has distinguished between the right to take interest on commercial loans, which are not in view here, and taking interest on loans made to a neighbor in his necessity. Risk capital owes the payment of interest. The needy brother, if he cannot pay, may not be threatened for either interest or even the loan itself. Such is the Biblical teaching.

6) Summary: thoroughly studied and courageously preached, the Bible opens compelling perspectives upon the economic relations which produce wealth, and into which wealth enters. It is easy to see that these texts, and many which might be added to them, simply focus on particular relationships the light shed by the obligation to love. Or, to put it another way, Biblical economics specifies what the Lord requires by saying: "So whatever you wish that men would do to you, do so to them; for this is the law and the prophets" (Matt. 7:12).

9. *The Biblical Summary*

What the Bible teaches concerning the obligations imposed by God in the gift of riches is summed up by St. Paul in words that explain themselves: "As for the rich in this world, charge them not to be haughty, nor to set their hopes on uncertain riches but on God who richly furnishes us with everything to enjoy. They are to do good, to be rich in good deeds, liberal and generous, thus laying up for themselves a good foundation for the future, so that they may take hold of the life which is life indeed" (I Tim. 6:17-19).

This summary of the Bible's perspectives on wealth should be preached, and pondered, and obeyed in the Church of Jesus Christ.

10. *Twin Mysteries:*

Concluding Observations

The aim of Christianity is fellowship with God.

The conditions for entering upon such fellowship are prescribed by the Holy Scriptures: "Jesus answered him (Judas, not Iscariot), 'If a man loves me, he will keep my word, and my Father will love him, and we will come to him and abide with him'" (John 14:23).

God gives us life and time for the sole purpose of beginning a fellowship with Him which will be consummated in eternity: "...and I heard a great voice from the throne saying, 'Behold, the dwelling of God is with men. He will dwell with them, and they shall be his people, and God himself will be with them...'" (Rev. 21:3).

God adds to life and time all other gifts of talent and goods, and provides in His Word instructions for making these into means for facilitating fellowship with Him. Mysteriously, and without explanation, He blesses many with poverty and some with riches. In both instances, God's design for promoting our fellowship with Him through the right use of His gifts may be frustrated by our disobedient use of them.

The Church has equal obligation to preach and teach the Word to poor and rich alike: "Hear this, all peoples! Give ear, all inhabitants of the world, both low and high, rich and poor together!" (Ps. 49:1-2). And this, as regards riches and poverty, is the substance of the Church's teaching: "The Lord giveth, the Lord taketh away; blessed be the name of the Lord" (Job 1:21); "And your ears shall hear a word behind you saying, 'This is the way, walk in it!'" (Is. 30:21).

In this light we make the following observations:

1. It is as difficult for the rich to acknow-

ledge that all their possessions are God's gifts as it is for the poor to recognize that their want is God's provision. Preaching both, and teaching them, will not be popular.

2. Materialism is as likely to characterize the poor as the rich—the one longing to acquire riches, and the other determined to hoard them.

3. Materialism may also characterize social reformers, even "Christian" social reformers, whose goals in practice often decline to crassly economic levels.

4. A noisy, pretentious concern for the poor may cloak a deep envy of the rich.

5. Intellectual reformers do not hesitate to use the poor as a lever upon the public conscience, not so much to alleviate poverty in itself as to attain their own manipulative ends.

6. Unlike some child psychologists, the Bible never hesitates to motivate behavior by promise of reward. Christ offers the rich young man what should have been a tempting alternative: "Sell all that you have and distribute to the poor, and you will have treasure in heaven..." (Luke 18:22). Surrender the temporal, and acquire the eternal—who offers a better bargain, and promises greater reward? It is some indication of the blindness induced by riches that this probably shrewd business man turned the Lord down. But the Word promises reward, both temporal and eternal, for obedience. So should the Church! The Bible also, of

course, guarantees grim "reward" for disobedience, especially on the Day of Judgment, and no one lays more emphasis upon that than our Lord Himself!

7. Our own materialism tempts us to interpret every Biblical reference to riches and to poverty in terms of material goods. It is evident, however, that the Word uses both "rich" and "poor" with far broader connotation, like:

a. The Biblical "poor" are those who know that their most basic needs for time and eternity *cannot* be met short of the Gospel, as the Bible presents the Gospel—namely, the power of God to make disciples out of rebels. These, whatever their material wealth, are the true poor to whom "the Gospel is preached" (Luke 7:22) and who gladly surrender all they have to God's service (like the man who commits all he has to buying a field where the Word is hidden—Matt. 13:44). Such "poor" are those who, because they know their own emptiness (however much they have in the way of goods), are "filled with good things" by the birth of the Lord (as Mary sings in her "magnificat," Luke 1:53). Such "poor" are those to whom "the kingdom of heaven" belongs because they know that God alone can give citizenship in that kingdom (Luke 6:20). These "poor" may be destitute or may be blessed in material possession, but their poverty is the only gateway to the eternal "riches" (Luke

16:11). Only God really knows who among us are such "poor," though their fellowship with Him will be suggested by their eagerness to put themselves and all they have at the disposal of His Word. The goal of the Church, in this context, is to alert us all to our *real* poverty!

b. Conversely, the Bible often derides the "rich" for their blindness, meaning those who are unaware of needs more profound than earthly goods can supply. These "rich" may possess great measures of wealth and talent, but they may also be materially destitute and greedily seeking riches—in either case their trust in riches or power or acclaim and their ambition is to acquire them. These are the "rich" sent "empty away" from the birth of Jesus, like those who filled the inn that first Christmas Eve and ignored the stable (Luke 1:53). These are the rich who are castigated by the Prophets, warned by the Lord, and condemned by the Apostles for putting God's gifts to their own service and trusting in the creature rather than in the Creator.

c. Unless the Christian bears these Biblical uses of the terms "poor" and "rich" well in mind, he is apt to confuse the instruction which the Word gives on wealth and poverty. The Bible does, indeed, speak directly to riches and poverty as such. But each reference in the Scriptures must be carefully tested as to what riches and which poverty are being discussed.

8. We conclude these observations with two illustrations of how a text may be confused by imposing materialistic interpretation upon its terms:

a. One of the most stringent Biblical admonitions concerning possessions occurs in St. Matthew's account of the Sermon on the Mount: "Therefore do not be anxious, saying, 'What shall we eat?' or 'What shall we drink?' or 'What shall we wear?' For your heavenly Father knows that you need them all. But seek first his kingdom and his righteousness, and all these things shall be yours as well" (Matt. 6:31-33).

Much is written about the Kingdom of Heaven. What does it mean to seek it first? And how, then, will food, drink, and clothing come tumbling after?

Quite simply, as is evident by definition, a kingdom exists where citizens swear allegiance to a king and undertake to obey his laws. All those who profess fidelity to God as their King and strive as loyal citizens to do His will constitute the Kingdom of Heaven in its temporal manifestation. Citizenship in God's Kingdom is not in conflict with political allegiance to any state which does not restrict liberty of worship and conscience. Indeed, the Christian is required by God to be a good citizen of such a nation. This is what the Lord implies by telling Pilate, "my kingdom is not of this world'' (John 18:36). Citizens of his Kingdom are interspersed among all nations. There is not, and cannot be, a geographical Kingdom of Heaven located among the world countries. God's Kingdom has no geography—and expands across all geography!

To seek, then, the righteousness of God's Kingdom means simply to do God's will with all our might and all our gifts and talents. And will this, then bring down a flood of riches? Yes, if it be remembered, now, that ''riches'' come in far more forms than just the material. But the Lord is speaking, in the text, directly to material goods: food, drink, clothing. How are these ''ours'' by first seeking the Kingdom's righteousness? Because all goods are, as it were, not really ours but simply on lease to us from the Giver *until we put them to His service!* Goods kept wholly for ourselves never do, really, pass from temporal lease to permanent possession. None of these is invested in heaven for permanent possession. We get lasting ownership only of those gifts we put to work here for the Kingdom, according to the King's Word: ''all these things shall be yours as well.''

b. ''Sell your possessions, and give alms; provide yourselves with purses that do not grow old, with a treasure in the heavens that does not fail, where no thief approaches and no moth destroys'' (Luke 12:33).

Some moralists call this a counsel of perfection. We think of it as fitting into the Biblical perspectives we have been outlining.

It is obvious, on reflection, that by no means all of God's gifts to us can literally be sold. Only material possessions can. Moreover, many of God's most obedient servants, like the Patriarchs, did not divest themselves of all their material goods. What, then, is meant here by "sell your possessions"?

To sell is to transfer title, done in consideration of a certain return. When, in consideration of a certain need, we place goods at the disposal of another, or place our time and talents in the service of another in love, we do fulfill the condition of the Lord's command to "sell" possessions. The purpose of goods is to serve. When we put the power lent us by great possessions into the service of justice benefitting those who need justice, this is as surely "selling" our goods as is turning them into money. Yes, let those who are influential so "sell" their possessions for the benefit of the needy. They will discover that the promise of reward is sure: "a treasure in the heavens that does not fail".

9. A final word: the Bible takes for granted that we know from experience how much "rich" and "poor" measure. The Word gives no definition of either. We know that the poor in a wealthy nation may be rich by contrast to the destitute in a deprived nation. We could stumble long and frustrate action indefinitely by demanding a definition of "rich"

and "poor" before putting ourselves and our gifts at God's command.

The needy become visible, not by definition but to the eye seeking out opportunities for stewardship. Whoever seeks fellowship with God by finding Him where service can be rendered to man will find the needy without ever defining them.

He or she is poor, right now, who needs something which another could give. He or she is rich, right now, who has something another needs. Often such needs can be measured, and met, in terms of material goods. As often, or perhaps oftener, human needs cry out for other forms of wealth, in compassion, concern, human interest, time, companionship, a smile, a word, a note, a call, a hand, a ride, a prayer.... By "selling" these the Kingdom is formed.

Chapter 13.

PARABLES FOR STEWARDS

Certain parables seem placed in the Scriptures just to teach stewardship. Parables like these:

A. *THE GOOD SAMARITAN:*
AWARE, CARE, SHARE

The parable of the Good Samaritan is familiar. A man was traveling from Jerusalem to Jericho. He is fallen upon by thieves who stripped and beat him and left him lying at the roadside half dead. A priest passed by, saw the victim, and crossed over to avoid him. So did a Levite. But a Samaritan, stranger to the victim by race and religion, saw him and had compassion on him. He bound up the man's wounds, put him on his beast, took him to an inn, and paid in advance for his care and keeping.

"Which of these three, do you think," the Lord asks, "proved neighbor to the man who fell among the robbers?" On hearing the

answer, "The one who showed mercy on him,"
Jesus said, "Go and do likewise" (Luke 10:25-
37).

First, one of the perpetual problems which
Christians face is illumined here. Between the
Samaritan and the victim there was no kinship
of religion or community. Yet Jesus clearly
commands just this kind of mercy. All Christians are obliged to reach out in care and
concern and practical assistance to all those
about them who are in need.

Second, this parable highlights three attitudes which believers must cultivate. They are:

1. Are you aware?

Three people passed by the man lying
beaten along the roadside. No doubt all three
saw him there. But two of them were not
aware, somehow, that here was human need
crying out for their help. Perhaps they were too
busy with their own affairs, or with those of
formal service to God. Whatever the explanation, they were not aware.

It is a question which Christians must
persistently put to themselves, both individually and in their meetings together: are we
aware of the needs about us? Do we see with
the eye of love what cries out for our attention?
In fact, do we want to see need and hear cries of
distress?

2. Do you care?

Two of those who passed by the man at
the roadside may have been aware, but did not

care. They felt no compulsion to assist. They heard no mandate of conscience. They declined to be neighbors.

From becoming aware to starting to care can be a difficult step. All kinds of reasons might be advanced why needs of which we have reluctantly become aware cannot really be met.

The parable passes no judgment on the two who either were not aware, or did not care. It only pronounces blessing on the one who did. The inference is unmistakable, and the command reinforces it: God requires caring, a caring that overcomes whatever obstacles may be posed against service.

3. Will you share?

The Lord has only one answer to this question: "Go and do likewise!"

Those who are of God must be neighbors to any who is in need of whatever God has given them to share with others. Christians *must* be good stewards!

B. *THE VINEYARD:*
FOR THOSE WHO DO NOT CARE

The prophet Isaiah tells of a vineyard planted on a very fertile hill. Its owner did all that one can do to prepare that vineyard to produce choice grapes. But it produced only wild grapes. And in his disappointment, the owner declares that he will destroy that vineyard and make it a wasteland where only briars and thorns will grow (Is. 5:1-6).

The same theme is taken up by our Lord, and reported in three of the Gospels (Matt. 21:33-46; Mark 12:1-12; Luke 20:9-19).

In each instance, it is clear that by the vineyard is meant the Church. For her the Lord has done all that can be done to insure the fruits of obedience and service. He has planted. He has preserved. He has sent prophets and teachers to instruct in His ways. He has given His Son that the guilt of the Church might be washed away. And what then does He ask of us? The obedience summed up in the love of God and neighbor.

It is our duty to distribute the fruit of the vineyard to those in need. The role of the vineyard is to provide fruit for such distribution. And the absence of such stewardship is no little thing. The terrible punishment foretold by Isaiah did fall upon fruitless Israel, and does fall upon fruitless 'christians' throughout history: "Do not be deceived; God is not mocked, for whatever a man sows, that he will also reap. For he who sows to his own flesh will from the flesh reap corruption; but he who sows to the Spirit will from the Spirit reap eternal life" (Gal. 6:7-8).

Hear then the conclusion of the matter, an admonition to the Church and mandate to the individual: "Let us not grow weary in well-doing, for in due season we shall reap, if we do not lose heart. So then, as we have opportunity, let us do good to all men, and especially to those who are of the household of faith'' (Gal. 6:9-10). "For He will render to every man according to his works: to those who by patience in well-doing seek for glory and honor and immortality, He will give eternal life; but for those who are factious and do not obey the truth, but obey wickedness, there will be wrath and fury'' (Rom. 2:6-8).

C. *THE GOOD SAMARITAN: ANOTHER LOOK*

A man traveling from Jerusalem to Jericho falls among thieves.

They rob and beat him, leaving him half dead at the roadside.

A priest hurries by, perhaps late for the time of sacrifice. He ignores the bloody figure in the ditch. So does a Levite who next comes by. Two religious professionals neglect the love of neighbor which they profess.

But a stranger, a Samaritan, one of a people alien to the beaten man, pauses, bends to dress the man's wounds, hoists him on his donkey, takes him to an inn, and pays in advance for his care.

All this is a story told 'round the world: the parable of the Good Samaritan (Luke 10:25-37), as recounted, also, above.

But has it become so familiar that you do not notice that the question which provoked the parable is not the question which our Lord answers?

The discussion began over eternal life. How

shall we inherit that most desirable of all blessings? A lawyer wants to know: "And behold, a lawyer stood up to put him to the test, saying, 'Teacher, what shall I do to inherit eternal life?' "

Jesus asks him what the Law requires, and the lawyer knows: to love God above all and our neighbor as ourselves.

Jesus commends his answer and adds, "Do this and you will live."

"But he, desiring to justify himself, said to Jesus, 'And who is my neighbor?'"

This is strange language. How "justify himself"? For what?

We know from our own experience. What we mean to justify by complicating the definition of "neighbor" is our own behavior in doing what the priest and the Levite did. We mean to leave the definition of "neighbor" so vague as to justify passing by many who lie beaten on life's roadsides. And we mean to substitute the delight of talk for the difficulties of obedience. The lawyer indeed means to "justify" himself —and us.

This then is the question shrewdly posed for the afternoon's leisurely exploration with the "Teacher": just who is my neighbor? That is, who is the one I must love as I do myself? Not everyone, surely? Least of all a stranger or alien? By what marks shall I know him? Puzzles enough for an endless delay in actualizing love.

But the Lord brushes such speculation aside. He is a Teacher who aims at action: "*Do this...and you will live*"!!

After telling the immortal story, Jesus quietly rephrases the lawyer's question. He does not say, "There, now you see who your neighbor is—not the priest, not the Levite, but the beaten stranger..."

No, He rephrases the question in a way which can no longer be endlessly refined, disputed, and thus evaded: "Which of these three, do you think, proved neighbor to the man who fell among the robbers?"

What was to be a long afternoon's idle talk ended abruptly. The lawyer was obliged to say: "The one who showed mercy on him."

And the clever would-be disputant was then dismissed with a curt, "Go and do likewise"! Why waste time discussing how we will know who our neighbor is? Just go and *be* "neighbor" to someone, to anyone, in need. Let the needy find his neighbor in you.

Drop the talk. Cut the chatter. Take God's gifts of time, money, goods, talents, counsel, a listening ear, a helping hand...out there where someone can use them.

To love a neighbor as yourself means simply to *be* a neighbor whenever and wherever you can.

Who is the neighbor?

Each of us is—or ought to be!

D. *GIVE AND FORGIVE*

"Give us this day our daily bread, And forgive us our debts, as we forgive our debtors" (Matt. 6:11-12).

A parable may be drawn from these familiar lines, taken from the prayer which the Lord instructs all Christians to use: "Pray then like this..." (Matt. 6:9).

Notice the play on words: "give" but "forgive".

The prefix "for" has the force of "not" here, of negation, of blotting out. We are asking God to "give" us all that we need for daily life, but "not" to give us the debit against our account which such giving lays upon us. *Give* us the bread, we pray, but *not* the debt which taking it should put upon us: give and forgive.

We need from God all that sustains daily life, all that makes it comfortable and enables us to do our work and enjoy our play. The Lord invites us to ask "Our Father" for all this. And He commonly gives far more than we know how to ask. This is why the prayer is made very simple: "daily bread" covers the needs we know and countless others of which we are completely unaware.

But this we do know, or should: we are far from using all His gifts in His required service, namely in the loving of the neighbor as ourselves. The debt we incur by accepting His gifts must needs be forgiven, and at once: we pray "give" and "forgive" in the same breath. Too much of what we are asking for will end up on the altar of self—or even of Satan.

The words flow easily enough...give...forgive. Who knows how often we have mouthed them?

But the Lord, whose prayer this is, obliges us to take upon ourselves a pledge: "as we forgive our debtors".

And who are they?

They must be those who bear the same relation to us that we bear to God: recipients of "daily bread" at our hand.

We acquire "debtors" just as God acquires them, by doing good. We put others in debt to us by doing for them what we ask God to do for us: give us what we need! as we give others what they need!!

The command to love the neighbor as ourselves means to make debtors. How else shall we be able to keep our part of the prayer's pledge, "as we forgive our debtors"?

Two obligations are implied by the pledge we say so readily:

1. That we make debtors by our stewardship, and

2. That we exact no compensation from them in return, not even thanks or appreciation.

Then we can pray, "Forgive us our debts, as we forgive our debtors."

The Lord stresses this relationship: "forgive, and you will be forgiven" (Luke 6:37).

The Lord emphasizes this solemn truth in another familiar story—which follows.

E. *SIMON'S SURPRISE*

Simon the Pharisee invited the "Teacher" to dinner. Whatever he may have expected in the way of good talk, he certainly did not anticipate what he was going to hear about himself. (Luke 7:36-50).

The Lord came to dinner.

While He was sitting at the table, "a woman of the city, who was a sinner" slipped in among the guests. Saying nothing, the woman "began to wet his feet with her tears, and kissed his feet, and anointed them with the ointment" which she had brought with her.

The Pharisee was disappointed. He thought that he had invited a "prophet" to be his guest, but this "Teacher" was apparently quite unaware of how unsavory was the character of her who was touching Him. A wasted evening after all, Simon was probably thinking, for, "If this man were a prophet, he would have known who and what sort of woman this is who is touching him, for she is a sinner."

Thus will men prescribe how God ought to behave—if only He were as "wise" as we, in our own sight, are!

But the Teacher was more of a prophet than Simon could possibly have surmised, and He breaks into Simon's reverie with what will become a scathing rebuke: "Simon, I have something to say to you...."

Unaware of what lies ahead, Simon asks, "What is it, Teacher?"

And the Lord begins to talk of debts and debtors—the theme we have just considered in the Lord's Prayer.

"A certain creditor had two debtors: one owed five hundred denarii, and the other fifty. When they could not pay, he forgave them both. Now which of them will love him more?"

Like the lawyer asking "Who then is my neighbor?" Simon walks into the trap from which there will be no escape. He says, "The one, I suppose, to whom he forgave more."

Whereupon Jesus lists the ways in which the woman had served Him in courtesies which Simon had callously neglected: Simon had not given Him, as custom required, water to wash His feet before dinner—the woman had supplied the lack with her tears. Simon had greeted Him with no kiss, as courtesy required —the woman had kissed His feet. Simon had provided no oil with which He might groom His hair and beard—the woman had anointed His feet with ointment.

She had in short, shown Him much love; Simon very little.

But the love we show reflects the love we have received. The debts we create by giving, and then forgive, measure our debts against

God which He has graciously forgiven: "Therefore, I tell you, her sins, which are many, are forgiven, for she loved much; but he who is forgiven little, loves little."

Those who create and then forgive few debtors by acts of love are, in fact, forgiven few of the immense range of debts we owe the Father. An absence of love for the neighbor betrays an absence of entrance upon the forgiving love of God.

The believer has a dual concern in all of his efforts to steward his blessing.

1. That, as God commands, the needy shall be satisfied with the gifts which He has entrusted to the stewardship of others for this purpose, and

2. That a generous heart testifies to a forgiven sinner, while a stingy heart betrays its own hardness.

F. *APPRENTICESHIP CHRISTIANITY*

"I am the way, and the truth, and the life..." (John 14:6).

Have you ever wondered why the Lord puts this order—way, truth, life—on His answer to Thomas' question?

The Lord had said to His disciples that He was going away. Thomas speaks for them all in asking: "Lord, we do not know where you are going; how can we know the way?"

Thomas thought that knowing comes first, and then going the right way follows. So, often, do we. A few years ago a book based upon this text was issued by several authors who tried to improve upon the Lord's teaching method by revising His order: they made it into "the truth, the way, and the life". But that is not what the Lord says, and it is not, therefore, what He means. Jesus is talking about apprenticeship Christianity, where doing precedes understanding.

Our Lord's heavenly Father destined Him to be raised in a carpenter's family. So, at least, is the tradition regarding Joseph. And carpentry, like most skills, can be talked about endlessly, but is really learned only by doing. Oh yes, the master carpenter tells the apprentice what to do, but the apprentice comes to knowing carpentry only by doing it. That makes all the difference between a sagging door hung by a novice and a neatly fitted one hung by a craftsman. The novice knows *about* carpentry; the master *knows* carpentry! This is true about most of living. First the doing, under guidance, and then the understanding. First the way; then the truth!

Remember that our Lord was, not predestined by His Father to birth where we might have expected Him, say into Herod's palace or a Scribe's scholarly abode. He was born, by divine design, into a laboring man's dwelling. He draws, in all His teaching, upon examples taken from Everyman's daily life.

It is entirely in keeping with His upbringing

by Joseph and Mary, according to God's pre-destined intent, that our Lord precedes understanding with doing. He sets the *way* before the truth! His hermeneutic (that is, His method of interpretation and understanding) is an apprenticeship hermeneutic. And it is an Everyman's hermeneutic. Open to all who believe. Not reserved for the learned, or the wealthy, or the powerful, or the famous. Quite the opposite, really: "And the common people heard Him gladly" (Mark 12:37). To all who, like Jesus' own disciples, learned their work by doing it, He quite naturally would say: first the way, then the truth of understanding, and in these the true life. Apprenticeship Christianity.

Oh yes, like the master craftsman, the Lord offers guidance for finding the right way. The Psalmist pointed that out centuries ago: "Thy word is a lamp to my feet and a light to my path" (Ps. 119:105). Peter said it, too: "Lord, to whom shall we go? You have the words of eternal life" (John 6:68).

The Lord's word-order is fundamental: first the way; then the truth grasped by our understanding; and, in these, the discovery of new life: I am the way, and the truth, and the life.

One more thing Christians must observe: Jesus says, "I am...."

We never seek, or walk, the way alone. He is the very Word that sheds light upon the path: "In the beginning was the Word, and the Word was with God, and the Word was God...In him was life, and the life was the light of men'' (John 1:1, 4). Those who come to understand the Word by doing it on the way of, and to, life, find that He has been joined with them on the way: ''If a man loves me, he will keep my word, and my Father will love him, and we will come and make our home with him'' (John 14:23). This blessed discovery of the presence of Jesus and His Father in the Word which guides our feet along the way is no doubt what ''understanding'' the truth really means. That is, we understand the Word by standing-under the Word as it illumines our path. And in such standing-under we have Jesus as companion, for He too came to walk the way set by His Father's will: ''I seek not my own will but the will of him who sent me'' (John 5:30).

Those who walk the way of obedience, that is the way of love to God and for neighbor made manifest in deeds, discover that Jesus Christ is, indeed, the way, the truth, and the life: ''I have been crucified with Christ; it is no longer I who live, but Christ who lives in me; and the life I now live in the flesh I live by faith in the Son of God, who loved me and gave himself for me'' (Gal. 2:20).

Chapter 14.

STEWARDS IN THE WELFARE STATE

Progress follows vision.

Those who aspire to participate in the Lord's designs for His Church must dream a little, must extend their reach beyond their grasp. Look up! Look around! Look ahead! Vision is an active function of a Body which is in league with the most progressive force in history, the power of the risen Lord: "having the eyes of your hearts enlightened, that you may know what is the hope to which he has called you, what are the riches of his glorious inheritance in the saints, and what is the immeasurable greatness of his power in us who believe..." (Eph. 1:18-19).

Vision taps that power, when it is vision bent upon obedience to the Head of the Church, whom God raised from the dead, "and made him sit at his right hand in the heavenly places, far above all rule and authority and power and dominion, and above every name that is named, not only in this age but also in that which is to come; and he has put all things under his feet and has made him head over all things for the church, which is his body, the fulness of him who fills all in all" (Eph. 1:20-23).

You cannot hope too much, envision too grandly, anticipate beyond His competence to bless. Therefore, in this chapter, we urge you to think big! In so doing, you are simply forging practical dreams for the extension of His hands, His eyes and ears, and His willing feet into greater and greater ranges of service.

Think on things like these:

A. *THE CHURCH AND THE WELFARE STATE*

We live in the era of the welfare state.

The Church is largely responsible for the coming of the modern welfare community. The Church could be largely responsible for purging welfare of its faults and disappointments. That is, if enough believers caught the vision.

If the Church is to amend some of the defects of welfare, she will do so through her diaconates.

If the believer is to assist in this purging of welfare-system deficiencies, it will best be done through prodding the deacons to catch the dream.

We begin by observing that the Church brought about the welfare state in two ways:

1. As we have seen, the Word which the

Church proclaims demands charity and justice for the poor. As this Word has permeated at least the Western world, an alerted public conscience has demanded public welfare. The Church is the parent of the welfare community.

2. But the Church did not, and perhaps in some respects could not, measure up to her own ideals. Not all the starving were fed, not all of the homeless given shelter, not all of the oppressed and exploited relieved. The cries of the needy ascended to heaven. The Lord answered with the welfare state. The government undertakes to do what the Church demands and then fails to achieve by herself.

Thus the Church is, both by commission and by omission, author of the welfare state. Christians start from here. Government has undertaken to do what conscience, tutored out of the Scriptures, demands but fails, through the Church, entirely to achieve.

It is futile, now, to argue long over the rights and wrongs of the welfare state. History will not reverse itself.

What is important, with an eye on tomorrow, is to discern what constructive relations may be developed between alert churches and public welfare. And it is immediately obvious that diaconates are uniquely qualified to amend what are commonly perceived as defects in the welfare system. Consider items like these:

1. The Christian knows that all goods come

from the hand of God. How stimulating for the needy welfaree to know that! How sobering for the chiseler! To know that God in heaven, looking down upon distress and responding to its cry, gives! This is exactly what welfare *is!* God's giving! You know that, but are you saying it? Are you teaching critics of the welfare system that God alone provides? That He is basic to welfare, and that without His Fatherly care neither birds of the air nor man nor beast would eat at all: "Look at the birds of the air: they neither sow nor reap nor gather into barns, and yet your heavenly Father feeds them. Are you not of more value than they?" (Matt. 6:26). God alone makes welfare possible. And this must always be known and said, even though under normal circumstances both He and we prefer that bread be given from above by way of our work here below: "Let the thief no longer steal, but rather let him labor, doing honest work with his hands," says St. Paul, though we must not neglect what follows: "so that he may be able to give to those in need" (Eph. 4:28). The needy, whom the Lord supplies through the work of others, will ever be with us (John 12:8). Public welfare is one of the Lord's vehicles of provision for the needy as He also provides for the birds of the air. The needy should know this! So should the rest of us!

2. The state, however, appears in welfare as a neutral agent. Welfare workers may, or may

not, take an interest in pointing recipients to the original Giver. This fact should burden the heart of the believer, of the deacon, and of the Church. And becomes a driving incentive for churches to get involved in the welfare system. Let God be properly honored, and thanked, for checks which come from the state but bear the return address of heaven! This is the basis for your interest in infiltrating the welfare process.

3. The state has no incentive to involve churches as witnesses to the largesse of their Lord. But the state has an interest in efficiency, and economy, and getting the most out of every welfare dollar. And here the Church finds its lever! Welfare is notoriously the victim of what must be generalized regulations, made to apply to everyone and therefore applicable precisely to almost no one. Justice in the abstract, which is the only way that justice can be sought through legislation, comes in practice to be in-justice, often, in the concrete. Some recipients get more, or other, than they need; some get less, even much less; while others are constant-ly tempted to "beat" the system in every way they can. Overburdened and usually unappre-ciated case workers struggle between bureau-cracy and reality, frustrated by both. Many do heroic work against sometimes crushing odds. How much they could use the steady hand, firm faith, and constructive vision of the Church! Is such a combination impossible? For-

bidden by the separation of Church and state? All depends upon how big you are willing to dream, and to work, and to hope, and to pray! Who holds "all authority in heaven and on earth" (Matt. 28:18)? Your Lord, or the state? What have you asked Him, and trusted Him, to do about welfare lately? He has given you every incentive to break, somehow, into the system!

4. Welfare, now, is commonly impersonal. Instead of creating community, it tends to destroy it. The case worker can rarely provide the personal touch which the love of Christ incites the Christian to radiate. How much more the welfare system, just as it is, could do for uniting the needy with the rest of society if the money and the assistance were given in the name of our common God and Father! Churches could see to that, if welfare were somehow administered with your help! Even if you only went along with the case worker, and stayed behind to round out what he or she does in the neutral name of government. Have you ever thought of that? It will be probably your best chance of worming your way into an otherwise crumbling public diakonia.

Yes, we think of deliberate strategies. Your goal is to restore charity to the Church which alone is capable of administering genuine diakonia! Perhaps you begin by tagging along, and staying to add in goods, or dollars, or teaching, or listening to whatever love senses is lacking in the welfare program as it applies to this particular person or family. Perhaps, if you do that well, your deacons can join other Christians already serving the Lord as professional case workers. And, if the Lord wills, in due season much of the welfare relief done in your parish or community is finally largely funneled through church hands. Separation of Church and state? Leave that to the Lord. If your church building catches fire, the tax-supported fire department will put it out. Why? For the common good. It is the common good which bridges the gap so artificially created by—we think—a misunderstanding of the First Amendment of the U.S. Constitution. And it will be the common good which chooses the efficiency of diaconal administration of welfare funds once you have demonstrated that only by individual handling of cases can welfare dollars do the most good. Try it! And with the Lord be the rest!

Try it? Yes, in ways like these:

1. Get to know all you can—all there is to know—about public welfare in your community. If yours is a rural congregation, or one in a small community where welfare is unknown, be prepared to offer assistance to diaconates serving in urban areas where for some families welfare is by now a way of life.

2. Get to know welfare case workers. Some may be members of your own congregation. Some, perhaps many, will be servants of the

same Lord you seek to honor. Find out how you might supplement their case work, both personally and with assistance in goods and funds.

3. You will no doubt discover that while welfare basically consists in "throwing money" at problems, there remains much left over for others to do. There might be cooperation with case workers in teaching right use of money, better ways of heating, of preparing food, of caring for household goods, and making clothes go a longer way. Christian women might, with prudent care for personal safety, participate in such training, either in the home or at the Church. Cooperation between welfare workers and collections of used clothing and staple foods maintained by volunteer workers at the Church opens doors.

4. Venture further by proposing pilot projects, in which the Church undertakes to assume the welfare load for selected families for a period of time. Do this under public scrutiny, with open books, and preconceived measures of efficiency. Let the figures speak. Let the families testify to what the touch of love adds to the welfare dollar. And thus undertake to convince the public mind that welfare need not be a "mess," if done in His name and through His—that is, your—hands! Do you know of a better gleam of hope to shed into a system of public charity no one likes but no one knows how to amend?

5. Do a study of what is so readily called "the separation of Church and state". Note that the First Amendment not only rejects a public "establishment" (that is tax-support) of religion, but equally prohibits the state from interference with "the free exercise thereof". Some day that second clause will re-open the doors of public education to Christianity. But for now let the believer observe that the so-called "wall of separation" is breached, as we have already observed, by the common good. Not only in the case of fire, but also when snow clogs the city streets leading to the Church— public vehicles plow them. Taxes are not collected from religious institutions. Police protect them, as does the military in time of war or riot. The common good binds Church and state together. And what greater contribution, now, to the common good than setting the welfare system back on its feet? Try it, and see!

6. Aim at the time when a certain share of welfare funds coming into your community are gratefully funneled through your hands. That this may, in the long run, oblige your congregation to join others in hiring a professional deacon or deaconess is all the more thrilling challenge!

Dream, Christian!

Your vision will never outreach God's grasp!

Chapter 15.

SOCIAL STRUCTURE AND HUMAN NEED: MARXISM AND LIBERATION THEOLOGY

There are those, as we have already observed, who believe that some social structures do impose poverty upon the many in the interests of the few. And they then conclude that the way to combat poverty is by way of revolutionary change of prevailing structures. This is the approach of Marxism. It is an approach more recently advocated by "liberation" theologians, who were once called "theologians of revolution". Many of these theologians speak out of the context of South America. They are quite willing to use Marxist analyses of social evil, and to suggest violent revolution as a way to eliminate human need.

The profile we have been developing in this volume, drawn we believe from the Bible, bears upon revolution as a means of structural change. Indeed, we think of universal stewardship as antidote to violent revolution.

We do believe that one crucial change in social structures contributes to human welfare at all levels of life, and that is the change from dictatorship and tyranny to the democratic state. But the violent, Marxist-oriented revolutions of this century have invariably been followed by extreme totalitarianism. The Communist state arising out of Marxist-inspired revolution is the ultimate in modern tyranny. Such structural change can never receive Christian endorsement.

Revolutions inspired by a Christian desire for liberty of worship have given birth to democratic institutions in the Netherlands, in France, in England, and in colonial America. Such structural change the Christian can endorse. It provides a political atmosphere in which the Church can breathe, preach, and freely witness in diakonia.

How, then, is stewardship an antidote to Marxist revolution?

Recall, first, that the office of deacon emerged in the Jerusalem Church in antithesis to a primitive communism. The Church began with an attempt to have "all things in common" (Acts 2:44, and 4:32). Very soon a whole class of members was neglected: "the Hellenists murmured against the Hebrews because their widows were neglected in the daily distribution" (Acts 6:1). The matter must have been serious, and the need extensive, because to meet it the Apostles recommended the appointment, not of one or two deacons, but of seven (Acts 6:3)!

Is this simply a passing matter only of historical interest to us?

We think not.

At issue is a very fundamental principle: the communal sharing of goods puts everyone at the mercy of the administrators. This is the basic defect of Communism. Where everyone theoretically "owns" everything, in practice no one can be assured of enjoying anything! And if this occurred within the Church, in the very flush of renewal after Christ's resurrection, how much more likely in the secular, totalitarian state! Indeed, how true of the Communist state, as the *Gulag* (prison system) of the Soviet union, and the refugees from Marxist states testify. Communism is not a viable alternative to ...

To what?

To stewardship, in a free society, done by Christians and churches inspired to serve!

What the Lord said to His people Israel on the lips of Moses, the Church now proclaims to the world: "But there will be no poor among you...if only you will obey the voice of the Lord your God, being careful to do all his commandments which I command you this day" (Deut. 15:4-5).

Revolution to achieve the political freedom which permits full obedience to the Lord's commandments? Yes, by all means!

Revolution to achieve elimination of the poor through the installation of a Marxist, or any other, tyranny? Not at all! This is the lesson taught by the experience of the Jerusalem Church, and exhibited unmistakably among those who now suffer under Communist dictatorship. Let the Church, and the young, and the liberation theologian take note!

Let it be conceded, in good faith, that the objective of liberation theology is humane. That the inspiration of such theology is the gross oppression of the weak and the poor by the rich and the powerful, often with the connivance of the Church. But the Word is sure: "But there will be no poor among you..." when? When the voice of the Lord is heard—from faithful, and in South America, courageous, pulpits. And when the commandments of the Lord are obeyed. And such obedience so far as the Body is corporately concerned, occurs in the stewardship of believers and the service of deacons.

In short, the believer stands on the firing line in the on-going struggle between using structures of freedom for the witness of service, and perverting social structures into Marxist totalitarianism through violent revolution.

By pursuit of Marxist rather than democratic political goals, liberation theologians neglect a fundamental Biblical truth. At issue in all political struggle is freedom to proclaim and obey the Word, not control of production and distribution of goods. The Word freely spoken, and heard unto obedience, focuses on the distribution of goods. But to put goods ahead of freedom for the Word is to lose both. So the Lord says to Satan: "Man shall not live by bread alone, but by every word that proceeds from the mouth of God" (Matt. 4:4, quoting Deut. 8:3). And that is why the Communist states may provide more food, better housing, warmer clothing, and improved health care than preceded them, only to find that all of these together do not satisfy man's hunger for freedom, that is, for opportunity to live in obedience to divine law.

The answer to Marxist structural change through violent revolution aimed at "dictatorship of the proletariat" was spoken by the Apostle Peter when Jesus asked His disciples if they, like the fickle crowd, would also desert Him. Peter replies, "Lord, to whom shall we go? You have the words of eternal life" (John 6:68). Revolution mounted to ensure the free preaching of these words is blessed. Revolution mounted to substitute another power for the creative force of His words only imposes the darkness of tyranny upon the soul.

But the Christian must remember that Marxism appealed to a world in which the Church did more speaking than obeying of the inspired Word. And some of those whom the Church never spoke for, and never served, turned in frustration to the "gospel according

to Marx''—and still do! And they create powerful states which threaten the freedoms hard
won for the West in Christian self-sacrifice.

Can human need be met while political freedom is preserved?

Yes, wherever stewardship perceives itself
as crucial alternative to Marxism!

Do your part, wherever you as Christian are
led.

What you do, in obedience to the words of
eternal life, opens up an alternative to liberation theology and Marxist revolution.

Chapter 16.

THE CHURCH AND INTER-NATIONAL COMMUNITY

The Church of Jesus Christ is one!

One Head implies one Body: "There is one body and one Spirit, just as you were called to the one hope that belongs to your call, one Lord, one faith, one baptism, one God and Father of us all, who is above all and through all and in all" (Eph. 4:4-6).

The Church has for centuries confessed her unity: "I believe one, holy, catholic Church...." So goes the Apostles Creed.

Notice that the Church universal is the object of belief, not of sight: "Now faith is the assurance of things hoped for, the conviction of things not seen" (Heb. 11:1). "I believe one, holy, catholic Church"—so millions of Christians have confessed across hundreds of years. So we join them today.

We know, however, that the Church universal does become visible in the local congregation. But the visible unity of the entire Church has never been achieved, and since the Reformation seems further removed than ever from accomplishment. Denominational divisions are not eclipsed by various national and international councils of churches. Nor has the breach between Protestantism and Rome ever been healed.

The visible institutional unity of the Church may never be achieved. Certainly in this era it remains an object of faith.

But while the institutional unity of the Church lags far behind our confession, a united deed witness opens a fruitful avenue to visible oneness.

Christian stewards, sacrificing themselves for the welfare of others, make visible individually the power of their faith. Viewed together, Christian stewards demonstrate the essential unity of the Church, bound by that faith.

The oneness of the Church becomes even more apparent in cooperative service rendered by countless congregational diaconates. Believers should push for such evidence of the Church's unity!

The Church has but one Savior, Head, Master, Lord. And because this is so, the Church is, in His holy sight, one Body. And therefore stewards' and diaconal hands are always His hands, no matter from which congregation they extend mercy. Stewards' and diaconal eyes are always His eyes, no matter where opened to need. Stewards' and diaconal ears are always His ears, whatever and wherever the cries they discern. Stewards' and diaconal feet bent upon His errands are ever His feet no matter from where and to whom they hasten.

Remember this, Believers!

Yours is the overt and visible testimony to the unity of the Body of Christ. When your service is joined with that of others, you make still more visible the oneness of the Church. All who lift their eyes to regional, national, and even international stewardship aspire to ever more visible witness to the one, holy, catholic Church! Stewardship pursued cooperatively becomes visible sinew binding the universal Church into objective unity.

Take inspiration from reflecting that the Church is the most enduring and most comprehensive of all institutions. No institution has lived longer and broken through more barriers of language, culture, and geography than has the Church. How better, then, to manifest this universal and enduring Body than in united witness by deed?

IN A NUTSHELL
"As each has received a gift, employ it for one another, as good stewards of God's varied grace: whoever speaks, as one who utters the oracles of God; whoever renders service, as one who renders it by the strength which God supplies; in order that in everything God may be glorified through Jesus Christ. To him belong glory and dominion for ever and ever. Amen" (I Pet. 4:10-11).

Life, time, talent and all that each of us has are gifts of God.

The right stewardship of all these gifts is what life is for.

The textbook to right stewardship is the Bible.

The school for instruction in the Bible is the Church.

The priesthood of all believers works through self-sacrifice to present to God the fruits of obedient stewardship.

That is what this book has been all about.

EPILOG

"Let me sing for my beloved a love song concerning his vineyard:
My beloved had a vineyard on a very fertile hill.
He digged it and cleared it of stones, and planted it with choice vines;
He built a watchtower in the midst of it,
And hewed out a wine vat in it:
And he looked for it to yield grapes..." (Is. 5:1-2).

He is still looking;
To the Church,
And to you, Christian Steward, whoever and wherever you are!

Notes

Notes

Notes

Notes

Notes

Notes

Notes